# SPORTS DEVOTIONS FOR TEEN BOY ATHLETES

60 DAILY DEVOTIONALS AND GUIDED PRAYERS TO HELP YOUNG CHRISTIAN GUYS BEAT PREGAME PRESSURE, BOUNCE BACK FROM MISTAKES, AND BUILD THE FAITH AND MENTAL TOUGHNESS TO LEAD ON AND OFF THE FIELD

## WONDER PLAYGROUND

WONDER PLAYGROUND PUBLISHING

# CONTENTS

**Disclaimer**

The content in this book is provided for educational and informational purposes only. While every effort has been made to ensure accuracy, the publisher and author make no guarantees regarding the completeness or reliability of the information presented.

The publisher and author disclaim any liability for decisions made or actions taken based on the information contained in this book.

# *INTRODUCTION*

## BEFORE THE WHISTLE BLOWS

## *YOU KNOW THE FEELING.*

It starts somewhere around the night before. Maybe it shows up as that tight, hollow sensation in your chest when you're trying to fall asleep. Maybe it hits in the locker room, when the pregame noise is everywhere but the only thing you can actually hear is the voice in your own head running every possible scenario of how tonight could go wrong. Your hands are a little cold. Your stomach won't stop. You keep bouncing your leg without meaning to, and you catch yourself staring at nothing.

Nobody tells you to feel this way. It just happens.

And here's the part that messes with a lot of athletes: this isn't even your first big game. You've been playing this sport for years. You've practiced hard. You know the drills. You've been in pressure situations before. And yet, there you are, heart hammering, brain spinning, wondering why you can't just calm down and feel ready.

Maybe you're also carrying something else on top of the nerves. Maybe there's a coach who has started questioning your role. A parent who watches every move a little too closely. A teammate who seems to have it all together when you feel like you're barely holding on. Or maybe the hardest pressure isn't coming from any of them — maybe it's coming from you. From the voice inside that keeps score on everything. Every missed shot. Every bad rep. Every game where you felt like you let someone down.

If any of that sounds familiar, this book was written for you.

# THE PART NOBODY TALKS ABOUT

Sports are incredible. That's the truth. There is almost nothing else in life that gives you the kind of electricity you get in competition. The camaraderie in a locker room. The feeling when a play comes together exactly right. The burn in your muscles when you've pushed past what you thought you could do. The pure joy of a win you fought hard for. Sports build something in you that's hard to find anywhere else — toughness, teamwork, discipline, and a kind of focus that carries over into everything.

But there's another side to it that doesn't get talked about enough.

The mental and emotional weight of being a competitive athlete — especially when you're a teenager — is real, and it's heavy. Pressure to perform. Fear of failure. The sting of a mistake that replays in your head for days. The exhaustion of trying to meet expectations that seem to shift every time you think you've reached them. The subtle but suffocating habit of measuring your worth by your stats, your playing time, your position, or whether the coach gives you a nod on the way off the field.

That weight doesn't go away on its own. And if you don't learn how to handle it, it can steal the joy of the very sport you love.

Here's what a lot of coaches, parents, and even pastors don't realize: teen athletes are not just struggling with the physical demands of their sport. They're struggling with deep questions about who they are. Questions that get tangled up with how they play.

*Am I good enough? Does my performance make me worth something? What happens to my value as a person if I have a bad game? If I lose my spot? If I get injured? If the coach stops believing in me?*

Those questions are not drama. They're not weakness. They're human. And they need real answers — not pep talks, not empty slogans, and definitely not more pressure dressed up as motivation.

# WHY IDENTITY IS THE REAL GAME

Here's the thing about identity: you're always building yours, whether you realize it or not. Every experience you have — every win, every loss, every remark from a coach, every moment of comparison with a teammate — is teaching you something about who you are and where your value comes from. The question isn't whether your identity is being shaped by sports. It is. The question is whether it's being shaped in a healthy way or a destructive one.

When your identity is rooted in your performance, your emotions follow your results. A great game makes you feel like you matter. A bad game makes you feel like you don't. A slump becomes an identity crisis. Criticism becomes a verdict on your worth as a person. That kind of emotional rollercoaster is exhausting, and over time, it doesn't just hurt your mental health — it actually hurts your performance. Fear of failure makes you hesitate. Overthinking makes you tighten up. Desperate attempts to prove yourself make you force plays that aren't there.

Performance-based identity creates the exact opposite of what you need to compete well.

Real confidence — the kind that holds up under pressure, the kind that lets you play free — doesn't come from your last game. It doesn't come from your coach's opinion, your stats, or your spot on the depth chart. It comes from knowing who you are at a level that goes deeper than any scoreboard.

That's where faith comes in. Not as a piece of soft inspiration stuck onto the side of your athletic life, but as the actual foundation beneath it. The kind of unshakable truth that doesn't rise and fall with your performance. The kind of identity that holds up when everything else is uncertain.

*"For I know the plans I have for you, declares the Lord, plans to prosper you and not to harm you, plans to give you hope and a future."* — **Jeremiah 29:11**

That verse doesn't say, "For I know the plans I have for you, assuming you play well this season." Your value in God's eyes is not a variable. It doesn't fluctuate based on game day. And once that truth settles into the deep places inside you — not just your head but your gut — it changes everything about how you compete.

# WHAT REAL MENTAL TOUGHNESS ACTUALLY LOOKS LIKE

Let's talk about mental toughness for a second, because that term gets thrown around a lot and it's often misunderstood.

A lot of people think mental toughness means not feeling anything. Shutting down emotion. Being a machine. Not letting anything get to you. Just grinding through, blank-faced and emotionless, like someone who has permanently turned off the human parts of themselves.

That's not mental toughness. That's just numbness with a sports metaphor attached to it.

Real mental toughness is different. It's not the absence of nerves — it's being able to compete well even when you're nervous. It's not the absence of fear — it's choosing courage in spite of fear. It's not pretending the pressure doesn't exist — it's learning to breathe inside the pressure and move forward anyway. It's the ability to take a hard hit, a bad call, a terrible mistake, or a devastating loss, and still come back. Still stand up. Still lead. Still play.

**Biblical mental toughness looks like this:**

It's the kind of peace that Paul wrote about — the peace that passes understanding, the kind that guards your heart and mind even when the situation around you is chaotic It's the courage that Joshua needed when God told him to be strong and not be afraid before a mission that seemed impossible. It's the resilience of David, who faced giants and wrote psalms in the same life. It's the self-control of an athlete in serious training — the kind Paul referenced in 1

Corinthians — who disciplines his body and keeps it under control for a purpose that matters.

That kind of toughness isn't built in a day. But it is built. That's exactly what this book is designed to help you do.

# THIS BOOK IS NOT YOUR TYPICAL DEVOTIONAL

Let's be real for a second. When some guys hear the word "devotional," they picture something their grandmother has on her nightstand — a little book with soft watercolor designs and vaguely encouraging sentences that feel like they were written for a completely different world than yours. Something you read dutifully, check off, and promptly forget.

This is not that book.

This book was built specifically for athletes in the middle of real situations. It was created for the guy who has a game on Friday and can't shake the nerves on Wednesday night. For the guy who just came off his worst game of the season and doesn't know what to do with that feeling. For the guy who is starting to suspect that his value as a person is tied too tightly to how he plays, and who wants to do something about it. For the guy who knows he should be spending more time with God but doesn't know how to make that work inside a life that is constantly busy, physically demanding, and emotionally complicated.

This book is a playbook. That word is intentional. A playbook is not something you just read once and stick on a shelf. It's something you return to. Something you apply. Something that helps you know what to do when the situation in front of you gets hard.

Every devotion in this book is designed to meet you in a real moment. Before a big game. During a slump. After a mistake that's still bothering you. When you're battling comparison, when discipline has slipped, when your confidence has taken a hit, when you're not sure how your faith connects to your sport at all. The Scriptures, principles, and action steps in these pages aren't decorative — they are practical tools for becoming a stronger athlete and a stronger young man.

# WHAT THIS BOOK WILL DO FOR YOU

Over the course of sixty devotions, you're going to work through the things that actually matter in your life as an athlete.

You're going to learn how to handle pressure — not by pretending it doesn't exist, but by understanding what it really is and where your stability comes from when it shows up. You're going to develop a stronger sense of who you are that doesn't crumble when your performance has a rough stretch. You're going to build habits of focus, discipline, and self-control that will make you a better competitor and a more trustworthy teammate and leader.

# *INTRODUCTION*

You're going to figure out how to bounce back. Because every athlete — no matter how talented, no matter how well-prepared — faces losses, mistakes, and setbacks. The ones who build something lasting are not the ones who never fail. They're the ones who know how to get back up, learn, and keep going without letting failure define them.

You're going to understand what it means to compete for something bigger than a scoreboard. That doesn't mean sports stop being important. They don't. Competition matters. Effort matters. Winning is genuinely great and worth working for. But when your sport becomes an act of worship — when you bring your best because it honors God and serves the people around you — it stops being something you do to earn your worth and starts being something you do from a place of purpose. That shift changes everything.

Each devotion in this book gives you a focused Scripture, a real-world situation you'll recognize, a practical principle to take into the week, a moment of honest prayer, and a challenge to put what you've read into action. These aren't long readings. They're designed to be read quickly and carried with you — into the locker room, into the weight room, into the moments that actually test you.

# A WORD TO THE PARENTS READING THIS

If you're a parent who picked this up for your son, thank you. And let me tell you what I hope this book does for him.

I hope it gives him a language for the things he's already feeling — the pressure, the fear of failure, the confusion about where his worth comes from — but hasn't had words for yet. I hope it builds in him a faith that is active, practical, and real in the context of his actual life, not just a Sunday morning experience that never touches the most demanding parts of his week.

I hope it helps him understand that struggling emotionally as an athlete doesn't make him weak. It makes him human. And that the path to genuine mental toughness, resilience, and confidence runs through honest faith, not around it.

I hope it helps protect him from one of the most common and painful traps that competitive athletes fall into: the trap of tying their identity so tightly to performance that they don't know who they are when the sport is taken away. Whether that day comes from injury, aging, or simply the end of a season, your son needs a foundation that holds. This book is one small but meaningful part of building that foundation.

Most of all, I hope this book gives you something to talk about together. Faith that stays in a book doesn't go anywhere. Faith that gets talked about, questioned, wrestled with, and lived out in real life becomes something that lasts.

# THE JOURNEY STARTS HERE

If you're the athlete reading this — here's what I want to say to you directly before you turn the page.

You don't have to have everything figured out. You don't have to already be spiritually mature or mentally bulletproof or somehow above the normal struggles of being a competitive teen athlete. You don't have to have a perfect game history, a perfect attitude, or a perfect faith. You just have to be willing to show up.

Every great competitor knows that the work done before the game — the preparation, the mental work, the character built in the quiet — is what determines who you are when the game is on the line. This book is part of that preparation. Not the only part. But a real part.

You are more than your last game. You are more than your stats. You are more than your mistakes, your losses, your playing time, or how impressive your highlight reel looks. You are a young man with a purpose, a future, and a God who is absolutely not done with you yet.

The pressure you feel? You can learn to use it instead of being buried by it. The fear? It doesn't have to run the show. The bad games, the slumps, the self-doubt — none of it gets the last word.

You were made for more than just surviving the pressure. You were made to compete with everything you've got, from a place of peace, with a strength that doesn't come from you alone.

*"I can do all things through Christ who strengthens me."* — **Philippians 4:13**

You've probably heard that verse a hundred times. Maybe it's stitched on someone's gym bag. Maybe you've seen it in an end zone. But don't let the familiarity make you miss what it actually says. Not some things. Not the easy things. Not the things you were already going to handle on your own. All things.

That includes the big game. The slump. The mistake you can't stop replaying. The moment you feel like giving up. The quiet Wednesday night when the nerves are already starting and the game hasn't even arrived yet.

All of it. He's in all of it.

**Let's get to work.**

# CHAPTER 1
# WHEN THE PRESSURE HITS

TRUSTING *God in Big Moments*

*"Be strong and courageous. Do not be afraid; do not be discouraged, for the Lord your God will be with you wherever you go." — Joshua 1:9*

## THE NIGHT BEFORE EVERYTHING

Picture this.

It's the night before the biggest game of your season. Maybe the biggest game of your life. You've been waiting for this one for months. Your team has been grinding for it since the first week of practice — the early-morning conditioning, the repetitions that made your muscles ache, the film sessions, the grind. All of it was pointing toward tomorrow.

You should be sleeping. The lights are off. Your bag is packed and sitting by the door. You know the time you need to be up. And yet.

Your brain won't stop.

The scenarios start running on their own, like a highlight reel you never asked for — except instead of your best plays, it's exclusively the worst-case versions of tomorrow. You see yourself missing the shot in the final seconds. You see yourself dropping the ball, fumbling the snap, false-starting off the blocks, losing the edge on a defender, throwing it right to the other team. You see your coach's face after. You see your teammates on the bench. You see the stands.

Your stomach does that thing. You know the thing — that low, hollow, twisting sensation that doesn't respond to logic. You're not actually running anywhere right now. You're just lying in bed. But your body is acting like the game is already happening, like you're already in the fire, like the danger is real and present and right outside the door.

So you flip over. Try the other side. Breathe. Check your phone — which, by the way, is definitely not helping — and put it back down. The thoughts come back. Now you're also thinking about the fact that you can't sleep, which is somehow making the pre-game anxiety worse, because everyone says you need good rest the night before a big game, and here you are at midnight with your heart doing its own cardio workout.

Sound familiar?

If it does, you're not broken. You're not weak. You're not spiritually immature. You're an athlete who actually cares about what you do. And that combination — caring deeply about something that is genuinely uncertain — is exactly the recipe for pressure.

Welcome to Chapter 1.

## PRESSURE IS NOT YOUR ENEMY (EVEN WHEN IT FEELS LIKE ONE)

Here's something that took a lot of athletes years to understand, and some never figure out at all: pressure is not a sign that something is wrong with you. Pressure is a sign that something matters to you.

Think about it this way. You don't feel nervous before you eat breakfast. You don't lie awake the night before a regular Tuesday practice. Pressure doesn't show up for things you don't care about. It shows up for the things you've poured yourself into — the moments where effort has been made, identity feels exposed, and the outcome is genuinely uncertain.

That's not a flaw. That's actually a kind of honor. The pressure you feel before a big game is, in a strange way, a tribute to how much you've invested. You care about your performance because you care about your team, your craft, your coaches, your goals. You care about doing well because you want to be excellent. That drive — that caring — is one of the best things about you as an athlete.

The problem isn't the caring. The problem is what the pressure does when it gets out of control.

When pressure spirals, it stops being motivation and starts being a prison. It moves from "I want to play well" to "I am terrified of playing poorly." And that shift — from want to fear — is where things start to go wrong in ways that are both mental and physical.

Your muscles tighten. Your movements become less fluid. You start playing cautiously, protecting yourself from the mistake rather than pursuing the play. You hesitate on decisions that should be instinctive. You're playing not to lose instead of playing to win. And ironically, defensively, fearfully trying not to mess up is one of the fastest ways to actually mess up.

*The athlete who plays free plays better. The athlete who plays scared plays small.*

That's not just a motivational slogan. There's real science underneath it. When the brain perceives threat — even imagined threat, like the threat of failure or embarrassment — it kicks the body into a stress response that is genuinely useful if you need to run from something dangerous, but terrible if you're trying to make precise athletic decisions. Your attention narrows. Your creativity drops. Your fine motor control suffers. Your timing is off.

In other words, fear of failure creates the neurological conditions most likely to produce the failure you were afraid of. The thing you most want to avoid, the excessive weight of trying to avoid it, actually makes it more likely to happen.

Which means the first step to playing better under pressure isn't trying harder. It's learning how to get out of your own way.

## THE OVERTHINKING TRAP

There's a specific kind of athlete — and you might recognize yourself here — who is naturally smart, naturally analytical, and naturally thorough. He prepares well. He studies the game. He thinks through situations. He is, in many ways, his own most demanding coach.

And in competition, that brain that serves him so well in practice becomes his biggest obstacle.

Because when you're competing, the thinking brain needs to step back and let the trained body do what it's been prepared to do. Skills that have been drilled into muscle memory don't improve with more conscious thought in the moment — they actually degrade. Ask any pitcher who has suddenly become terrified of hitting batters. Ask any basketball player who has started thinking about his shooting mechanics mid-game instead of just shooting. Ask any kicker who thinks too hard about the angle of his foot during a field goal attempt.

There's a reason coaches talk about playing instinctively. It's not anti-intellectual. It's recognizing that the cognitive overhead of trying to manually control your athletic execution in the middle of a game is a performance killer. You've already done the thinking — in practice, in film study, in preparation. Game time is the time to trust what you've built and let it run.

But fear makes that trust nearly impossible. When you're afraid — afraid of failing, afraid of embarrassment, afraid of letting someone down — your mind refuses to release control. It keeps jumping in, second-guessing, trying to protect you from the bad outcome it's already convinced is coming.

**Overthinking under pressure often looks like:**

Hesitating on plays you would normally make automatically. Changing your approach last-minute because of sudden doubt. Thinking about what your coach is going to say before the play is even finished. Mentally replaying a mistake from two plays ago while the current play is developing. Worrying about the final score before you're even at halftime. Trying to force a standout performance instead of just playing your game.

Any of that sound like your brain on a bad day?

The athletes who handle pressure best are not the ones who think the least. They're the ones who have learned to direct their thinking — to focus on the right things at the right times, and to release the things they can't control.

That's a learnable skill. And faith, surprisingly, plays a significant role in developing it.

# THE INVISIBLE WEIGHT: WHERE REAL PRESSURE COMES FROM

Let's dig a little deeper for a second, because the nervous stomach and the racing thoughts are symptoms. The actual root of performance pressure is something more fundamental.

Most athletes — most people — carry a hidden belief that goes something like this: My value as a person is connected to my performance.

Nobody sits you down and teaches you this directly. Nobody writes it on a whiteboard and makes you memorize it. But it gets absorbed through a thousand small signals over years of competing. It's in the way a good game earns praise and a bad game earns silence. It's in the way playing time communicates your ranking in the eyes of the people you respect most. It's in the way the team treats the star player and the way they treat the guy at the bottom of the depth chart. It's in the way wins produce celebration and losses produce tension that hangs around for days.

And slowly, quietly, athletes start to connect dots that should never be connected: how I play = who I am.

When that belief is operating in the background, the stakes of every competition become enormous in ways that go far beyond the sport itself. It's not just about this game anymore. It's about whether you matter. Whether you're good enough. Whether you deserve to take up space on the court, the field, the mat, the track. Whether you've earned the respect and affection of the people whose opinions you care about.

That is a crushing weight to carry into a game. And most athletes are carrying it without even realizing it.

It shows up in different ways for different guys. Some athletes become reckless — they're so desperate to prove themselves that they take ill-advised risks, try to do too much, force plays, and consistently go outside the team concept because subconsciously, individual success feels more urgent than team execution. Others become paralyzed — so afraid of a mistake that confirms their deepest fear of unworthiness that they shrink, hold back, and never quite play with the freedom they're capable of. Some guys cover the pressure with bravado, acting like nothing bothers them while internally they're in free fall. Some guys direct it outward as frustration — anger toward coaches, officials, or teammates that is really just displaced anxiety about their own performance.

Different expressions, same root. And until the root gets addressed, managing the pressure is just whack-a-mole — you push it down in one area and it pops up somewhere else.

*"Do not be anxious about anything, but in every situation, by prayer and petition, with thanksgiving, present your requests to God. And the peace of God, which transcends all understanding, will guard your hearts and your minds in Christ Jesus." —* ***Philippians 4:6–7***

This verse isn't just a pleasant thought to hang on your wall. It's a practical prescription for exactly the kind of anxiety that lives in a competitive athlete's chest the night before a big game. Notice what it says: in every situation. Not in the easy situations, not after the game is over, not in the comfortable and safe moments. Every situation. Including this one. Including yours.

The peace God offers isn't the peace of having no problems. It's peace that transcends the circumstances — peace that exists even when the stakes are high, even when the outcome is uncertain, even when the pressure is real. It's peace that doesn't make logical sense given what you're facing, which is exactly why Paul calls it peace that passes understanding.

That's available to you. Not just in theory. Right now, in the locker room, before the biggest game of your season, with your hands sweating and your thoughts running — that peace is available. But you have to know how to reach for it.

# WHAT FAITH ACTUALLY CHANGES

Let's be honest about something. Saying "just trust God" is advice that, without context, doesn't actually help much. Athletes have tried to do that. They've prayed before games, said the right words, tried to feel peaceful — and then still felt their heart rate go through the ceiling the moment the game started. And then felt confused, or guilty, or like their faith wasn't working right.

So let's get specific about what faith actually does and doesn't do when it comes to pressure.

Faith does not eliminate nerves. Even the most spiritually mature athletes feel nervous before big competitions. Nerves are a physiological response. Adrenaline is a real hormone. The physical experience of a racing heart and heightened awareness before competition is not a spiritual failure — it's a biological feature. Your body is gearing up. That same adrenaline, when channeled correctly, actually improves athletic performance. The goal is not to get rid of it. The goal is to not be controlled by it.

Faith does not guarantee a particular outcome. God is not a scoreboard manipulator. He is not more interested in whether your team wins this game than He is in who you are becoming through the experience of competing. The Christian life does not come with a promise of easy victories and favorable outcomes. It comes with a promise of presence — that God is with you, that He is working all things for your good, and that your value in His eyes has nothing to do with what the other team does in the fourth quarter.

What faith does change is the foundation you're standing on when the pressure comes.

When your identity is rooted in performance, every big game carries existential weight. This game determines my value. This game tells me who I am. This game will decide whether I'm worthy of being respected and loved. That's a crushing burden, and it's a lie — but it's a lie that feels profoundly true when you've spent years absorbing it.

When your identity is rooted in Christ, the game still matters — but it doesn't carry your worth. You can compete freely because the outcome doesn't define you. You can take risks because failure doesn't make you a failure as a person. You can give your full effort because you're playing from abundance instead of scarcity, from security instead of desperation.

That shift doesn't happen overnight. It's a process of repeatedly bringing your mind back to what is true about you before the scoreboard ever starts. But every time you make that choice — every time you consciously root your identity in something more stable than performance — the foundation gets a little bit stronger.

*You are not competing to earn something you don't have. You are competing from something you've already been given.*

Read that again and let it settle.

You are not playing to become worthy. You already are. You are not performing to earn your identity. You already have one — one that was established before you ever set foot on a field or a court, before your first stat was ever recorded, before anyone ever evaluated your athleticism or decided what position you deserved.

You are made in the image of God. You are known by name. You are valued not for your athletic output but for who you are. And no bad game, no slump, no mistake, no cut from a team can change that. It's the one thing in your life that cannot be taken from you by anyone else's decision or opinion.

When that truth becomes real to you — not just intellectually true, but lived and believed and felt in your chest — it fundamentally changes how you walk onto the field.

# JOSHUA AND THE WEIGHT OF THE MOMENT

There's a man in the Bible whose situation was about as high-pressure as it gets. His name was Joshua.

Joshua had just been handed the job of leading an entire nation into an unknown territory filled with fortified enemies, after following the most significant leader in Israelite history — Moses. The people were scared. The mission was massive. The stakes were higher than any sports competition you will ever experience. And Joshua was standing at the edge of it all, about to step in and lead.

You might expect God to open that conversation by explaining the full strategy. Breaking down the playbook. Giving Joshua a detailed map and a list of contingencies for every possible scenario.

He didn't.

Instead, God said: Be strong and courageous. Do not be afraid; do not be discouraged, for the Lord your God will be with you wherever you go.

Three times in one chapter, God tells Joshua to be strong and courageous. Why would God need to say that three times? Because courage is not a feeling that arrives fully formed and permanent. It's a decision that has to be made again and again in the face of a pressure that doesn't go away on its own.

And here is the crucial detail: God did not tell Joshua to be courageous because the situation wasn't hard. He told Joshua to be courageous because He was going to be with him in the middle of it. The courage was not based on the difficulty of the mission being minimized. It was based on the certainty of the presence of God.

That's the model. Not: there's nothing to fear because the stakes are low. But: there is reason for courage because you are not alone.

You are not alone on the court. You are not alone on the field. You are not alone in the moments when pressure wraps around your chest like a vise and your inner voice starts cataloguing everything that could go wrong. The God who told Joshua to be courageous because He was present is the same God who is present with you — in your locker room, in your warmup, in the first minutes of the first period when the nerves are at their peak.

Be strong and courageous. Not because the game doesn't matter. Not because you're guaranteed to win. But because you are not in this alone.

# WHAT CHRISTIAN MENTAL TOUGHNESS REALLY LOOKS LIKE

If you ask most people what mental toughness looks like, they'll describe something like a stone wall. Impassive. Hard. Unaffected. The athlete who never shows emotion, never flinches, never admits that anything is getting to him. The guy who always looks like he just drank a cold glass of invincibility.

That kind of toughness might look impressive from a distance. Up close, it's usually either a performance or a problem.

Because emotions don't disappear when you suppress them. They go underground. And underground emotions don't stay underground forever — they come out as blowups, as burnout, as the slow erosion of the joy that brought you to the game in the first place. The athlete who has walled off his entire emotional life in the name of mental toughness eventually has nothing left to compete for.

Christian mental toughness is not about being a wall. It's about being a foundation.

A wall repels everything. A foundation holds firm while everything presses against it. A wall has no flexibility — hit it hard enough in the right place and it cracks. A foundation has depth — the pressure can be enormous, and it still stands because of what it's built on.

Here is what real mental toughness looks like in a Christian athlete:

It is peace that holds under pressure — not because nothing can touch you, but because you know who holds you. It is the ability to feel the nervousness, acknowledge it honestly, and choose to act with courage anyway. It is the discipline to redirect your thoughts when they start spiraling — not to pretend you're not spiraling, but to recognize what is happening and intentionally bring your attention back to what is true, what is useful, what is in your control.

It is humility in success — not playing it cool as performance, but genuinely knowing that your ability is a gift and your success is something to steward and share. It is resilience after failure — not the artificial cheerfulness of pretending a loss didn't hurt, but the deeper conviction that who you are is intact even when the scoreboard isn't.

It is self-control in the emotional heat of competition — when a bad call makes your blood boil, when a teammate makes a mistake that costs you, when the momentum swings hard against you and the easy thing is to mentally tap out. That's the moment where real toughness lives. Not on the highlight reel, but in the decision to stay focused, stay disciplined, and keep competing when everything in you wants to either give up or blow up.

It is, above all, trust. Trust that God is present. Trust that your worth is secure. Trust that this moment — however it goes — is part of something larger than a box score.

*"I have learned, in whatever state I am, to be content. I know how to be abased, and I know how to abound: everywhere and in all things I am instructed both to be full and to be hungry, both to abound and to suffer need. I can do all things through Christ who strengthens me." — **Philippians 4:11–13***

Notice that Paul says he learned contentment. It wasn't a gift delivered instantly. It was developed through experience — through abasement and abundance, through difficulty and ease. That's how mental toughness works too. It is not a personality trait you either have or don't have. It is built over time, through pressure, through practice, through the consistent choice to root yourself in something unshakeable.

And note the progression. Paul describes going through circumstances that could easily have stolen his peace — imprisonment, persecution, lack of food — and yet having found a strength that was not his own. I can do all things through Christ who strengthens me. Not some things. Not the comfortable things. All things. Including this game. Including this pressure. Including this moment.

# PRACTICAL TOOLS FOR PRESSURE MOMENTS

Okay. Let's talk real, practical, usable stuff. Because this book is a playbook, and a good playbook isn't just philosophy — it's tools. Here are ways to actually engage with pressure when it hits.

**1. Slow the moment down with your breath.**

When pressure peaks, your nervous system is in overdrive. One of the fastest ways to physically interrupt a stress response is controlled breathing. This is not a spiritual hack — it's biology. Slow, deliberate, deep breaths activate the parasympathetic nervous system and begin to counteract the adrenaline cascade of the stress response. Before a big play, a free throw, a penalty kick, a serve: breathe In for four counts, hold for four, out for four. It takes about thirty seconds and it actually works.

Elite athletes do this. Military operators do this. Surgeons do this. It's not a weakness to need to regulate your nervous system. It's just intelligence applied to biology.

**2. Reset your attention to what you can control.**

Pressure loves to pull your attention toward outcomes you cannot control. The scoreboard. The crowd's reaction. What your coach thinks. Whether you'll play well enough to earn more playing time. Whether the other team's best player is going to have a breakout game. None of that is in your control, and the more mental energy you burn on it, the less you have for what actually is.

What is in your control? Your effort. Your focus on this play, this moment, this assignment. Your communication with teammates. Your attitude. Your discipline in the process.

The Stoics had a phrase for this — focusing on your sphere of control. The Bible has something similar: fix your thoughts. Do not let your minds go wherever fear takes them. Direct them intentionally. Paul puts it this way in Philippians 4:8 — think on what is true, honorable, right, pure, lovely, and admirable. In an athletic context, that means keeping your mind on what is true about who you are and what you are called to do in this moment, rather than on the spiral of what-ifs and worst-case scenarios.

**3. Speak truth before you perform.**

This is not the same as hyping yourself up with empty slogans. This is about taking the lies that pressure tells you and replacing them with what is actually true.

Pressure says: If you mess this up, you're a failure. Truth says: My worth is not determined by this play.

Pressure says: Everyone is watching and they're waiting for you to blow it. Truth says: I have prepared for this. I am not alone. I compete for something bigger than any single performance.

Pressure says: You don't deserve to be here. Truth says: God made me. He placed me here. He is with me right now.

That practice — identifying the lie, countering with truth — is not automatic. It takes practice, just like any other athletic skill. But it is one of the most powerful tools available to a competing athlete. What you say to yourself in the middle of pressure matters enormously.

**4. Pray briefly and specifically.**

Not a long eloquent prayer. Not a theological treatise. Just a direct, honest, short conversation with God in the moment.

God, I'm nervous. I need you right now. Give me peace and clear focus. Help me compete with everything I have, and remind me that my worth is in you no matter how this goes.

That's it. That's enough. God doesn't need your vocabulary to be impressive. He needs your heart to be honest. You can do that in fifteen seconds before the opening whistle, in a free throw routine, in the breath before a race starts.

And here's something significant: the act of praying before a performance is itself a theological statement. It is a practical acknowledgment that you are not the source of your own strength. That you don't go into this alone. That whatever happens, you are being held by something larger than the game. That acknowledgment, repeated consistently, does something to your confidence over time — it roots it in the right place.

**5. Play for effort and obedience, not outcome.**

This is one of the most freeing reframes available to a competing athlete. The outcome of a game involves many variables beyond your control — the other team's performance, officiating, weather, injuries, bounce of the ball, countless things you cannot manage. But your effort? Your obedience to your preparation, your role, your team concept? That is entirely in your hands.

When the goal is to control what you can control and give maximum effort and focus to that, the grip of outcome-anxiety loosens. You can play freely when your definition of success is not contingent on a scoreboard result but on whether you showed up fully and competed with everything you had.

This is not a philosophy of not caring about winning. Winning is great. Compete hard for it. But keep the bottom line in the right place: did I give what I had, did I play the right way, did I honor God and my teammates with the effort and attitude I brought? That's a bottom line you can actually achieve regardless of what the scoreboard says.

# PRESSURE IS WHERE CHARACTER IS BUILT

Here's something nobody told you when you signed up for this: the pressure is part of the point.

Not because someone is trying to torture you. But because character doesn't grow in comfort. Resilience doesn't form in the absence of adversity. Courage only exists in the presence of something to be afraid of. You cannot develop mental toughness in a context where nothing is difficult.

Every high-pressure moment in your athletic career — the big game, the late-game situation, the unexpected adversity, the competition that scared you — is also a formation opportunity. It is a moment in which something in you can either shrink back or grow forward. The outcome of the game will be forgotten in time. The character built or neglected in those moments goes with you everywhere.

Think about the athletes you admire most. Not just the most gifted, but the ones who actually became great. The ones who have the kind of competitive presence that makes you stop and pay attention. Almost without exception, those athletes went through pressure. Adversity. Hard seasons. Difficult moments. And they learned something in those crucibles that couldn't have been learned any other way.

You are in your formation years right now. The habits, the mental frameworks, the relationship with pressure that you develop as a teen athlete will follow you into everything that comes after. Not just your athletic career — but your work, your relationships, your family, your leadership. The young man who learns how to stay grounded under pressure becomes the adult who can handle the real pressures that life delivers.

James 1:2–4 puts it this way: Consider it pure joy, my brothers, whenever you face trials of many kinds, because you know that the testing of your faith produces perseverance Let perseverance finish its work so that you may be mature and complete, not lacking anything.

Testing produces perseverance. Perseverance produces maturity. Maturity is completion — becoming the full version of who you were made to be.

The pressure on game day is not just an obstacle to your performance. It is a test of your faith, and in that test, something is being built in you that matters more and lasts longer than any trophy you'll ever hold.

*The pressure you're feeling right now isn't here to defeat you. It's here to develop you.*

That reframe doesn't make the nerves disappear. But it changes what they mean. Instead of evidence that something is wrong, they become evidence that something is happening — something worth being part of, something that's developing you into someone stronger, more capable, more grounded.

Lean into it. Don't run from it. God doesn't put you in pressure moments so you can be crushed. He puts you in pressure moments because He knows what they're capable of producing in you if you bring your faith with you instead of leaving it in the parking lot.

# BEFORE YOU PLAY: A WORD FOR RIGHT NOW

If you're reading this the day before a game — or the day of — here's what I want you to hear, and I want you to actually hear it, not just read past it.

You have done the work. The preparation happened. Whatever your level of readiness, you have put in real effort to get to this point. The work is done. What's left is to compete.

The outcome of this game does not define you. It never has. Whatever happens on that field, court, mat, or track today, you will walk away the same person — a person who is known by God, loved unconditionally, and on a journey toward something bigger than any single scoreboard.

The nerves you feel are telling you that this matters to you. Let them. Don't try to make them go away — just don't give them the steering wheel. Feel the adrenaline, acknowledge it as the body gearing up to compete, and choose courage anyway.

You are not alone. The same God who told Joshua to be strong and courageous — not because the mission was easy, but because He was present — is the same God who is present with you today. In the locker room. In the warmup. In the first minutes when the pressure peaks. He is there.

Play free. Play your game. Give everything you have. Compete with purpose and peace and the fullness of the ability that has been placed in you.

And after the final whistle — win or lose — know that you played for something that outlasts the result.

That is what it means to be a Christian athlete. Not that you perform better because of your faith — though over time, you very well might. But that your faith gives you a foundation solid enough to compete without being controlled by fear. A peace strong enough to hold under pressure. An identity stable enough to survive both the best and worst games of your career.

That's available to you. Right now. Before the opening whistle.

Take it.

# A PRAYER FOR THIS MOMENT

*God, I'll be honest — I feel the pressure right now. My heart is beating faster than I want it to. I have fears about today, about how I'll perform, about what people will think.*

*So I'm bringing all of that to You. Not trying to dress it up or make it sound better than it is. Just laying it down.*

*Remind me right now that my worth is in You — not in the box score, not in the coach's opinion, not in a highlight play. You made me. You know me. You are with me in this.*

*Give me peace that doesn't depend on how today goes. Give me courage to compete freely and give everything I have. Help me play with the freedom of someone who has nothing to prove and everything to give.*

*And whatever the outcome — let me walk off that field knowing I competed for something bigger than a result.*

*I trust You with this. Amen.*

# THINK ON THIS

1. What specific fear do you carry into competition most often? What lie is underneath it?

2. How would you play differently if you were completely free from fear of failure?

3. What truth about your identity in Christ do you most need to hold onto the next time the pressure hits?

4. Who in your life models the kind of peace-under-pressure described in this chapter? What can you learn from watching them?

# GAME-DAY CHALLENGE

This week, before your next practice or game, do this:

Write one sentence on a small piece of paper or the notes app on your phone. Make it a truth statement about your identity — not about your performance. Something like: "I am made by God, known by God, and my worth doesn't depend on today's result."

Read it out loud before you compete. Not as a magic formula — but as a deliberate act of redirecting your foundation. Do it once this week. Then decide if it made a difference.

Bonus: the next time you feel the anxiety spiral starting, try the four-count breathing method and a fifteen-second prayer before you keep going. Notice what shifts.

# CHAPTER 2
# MORE THAN THE SCOREBOARD

FINDING *Your Identity in Christ*

*"See what great love the Father has lavished on us, that we should be called children of God! And that is what we are!"* — **1 John 3:1**

# AFTER THE FINAL WHISTLE

You know what's interesting about the car ride home after a bad game?

Nobody has to say anything for it to be brutal.

The silence does enough on its own. Maybe your parent is trying to be supportive and just doesn't know what to say. Maybe they're genuinely fine — maybe the game really doesn't bother them the way it's bothering you. Either way, you're in the passenger seat watching the streetlights go by, and your brain is already running the full replay. Every missed assignment. Every moment you were a half-second late. Every play where you had a chance and didn't convert. The final score sitting in your chest like a stone.

And the worst part is that it doesn't feel like the game is bothering you. It feels like you are bothering you.

There's a difference, and it matters. When a bad game feels like a bad game — frustrating, disappointing, something to learn from and move on — you can process it and come back the next day ready to work. When a bad game feels like a verdict on who you are as a person, that's a different beast entirely. That's the version that follows you to bed, hangs around at school on Monday, and makes it hard to walk into practice with your head up.

Most athletes have been there. Many are there more often than they'd admit. And almost none of them have been told the truth about why it hurts so much.

The reason bad games can feel so personal is because, for a lot of athletes, they are personal. Not because sports are silly or emotions are dramatic, but because somewhere along the way, the sport stopped being just something you do and started being something closer to who you are. Your identity got wrapped up in the jersey. Your sense of value got tied to your stats. Your confidence started rising and falling with your performance, like a stock price that nobody told you was supposed to be stable.

This chapter is about that.

Not to make you care less about sports — caring about your craft is actually good and we're going to talk about why. But to help you understand how performance-based identity works, why it's so common, why it's so destructive, and what a better foundation looks like.

Because you deserve to play free. And right now, if you're honest, you're probably not playing as free as you could be.

# HOW SPORTS BECOME IDENTITY: THE HONEST VERSION

Nobody sits down at age twelve and consciously decides, "From now on, I'm going to base my entire sense of self-worth on how well I play this sport." That's not how it happens. It happens quietly, gradually, through a thousand small experiences that each seem normal on their own.

Think about the math of a serious athlete's life. If you're playing at a competitive level, you're probably spending fifteen to twenty-five hours a week — sometimes more — in direct connection to your sport. Practice, games, travel, film, weight room, individual training, visualizing, watching highlights, talking about it with teammates, thinking about it in class when you're supposed to be doing other things. Your closest friendships are probably with people on your team. Your schedule is organized around game days and practice times. Your family's weekends are built around your season.

Sport is not just something you do. It is the central organizing structure of your life.

And into that structure, feedback flows constantly — a constant stream of evaluation, comparison, and response that is hard to keep from internalizing. Your coach tells you what you did right and what you did wrong. Your stats are recorded and visible. Playing time tells you exactly where you rank. Postgame conversations, social media responses, the look on your parent's face driving home — all of it communicates something about how you performed, and by extension, in the way your brain has quietly learned to interpret it, how you are.

When you play well, people respond warmly. Coaches are encouraging. Teammates are excited. Parents are proud and happy and easy to be around. When you play poorly, the warmth cools. Coaches are less affirming. Teammates get frustrated. Parents go quiet or say things that, however well-meaning, land harder than intended. The emotional weather around you follows your performance, and you're not imagining it. It actually does.

So here's what your brain starts learning, even if you never consciously notice: performance earns warmth. Excellence earns attention. Mistakes earn disapproval. Playing well makes people treat you better. Playing poorly makes people treat you with less enthusiasm.

And from there, the leap is not hard to make: performance determines worth.

It's not a rational conclusion. But it's a very human one. And once that equation is operating in the background of your mind, every game carries more weight than it should, and every bad performance cuts deeper than it ought to.

*You didn't choose to build your identity on sports. It just sort of happened. But you can choose something different.*

That's the honest version of how athletes end up in this place. And it's important to say it plainly, without judgment, because the first step to building a better foundation is recognizing that the current one isn't as solid as it might look.

## WHEN THE SCOREBOARD STARTS RUNNING YOUR LIFE

Let's look at what performance-based identity actually produces when it's fully operational. Because it has a signature — a recognizable pattern of thinking and feeling that a lot of athletes walk around in without ever having a name for what it is.

The defining feature is that your emotional state follows your performance. Not just in the minutes after a game — that's normal; everyone feels good after a win and bad after a loss for a little while. The performance-based identity problem is when it stays. When the good game high lasts for days and the bad game hangover does too. When your confidence is directly proportional to how you played last. When you're walking into school on Monday a fundamentally different version of yourself depending on what happened on Friday night.

Other patterns that usually come with it:

Praise becomes more than encouragement — it becomes fuel you run on. When a coach says something positive, it doesn't just feel good. It feels necessary. Needed. Like air. And when the praise is absent, when a coach goes quiet or seems to have focused his attention elsewhere, there's a hunger for it — a restlessness, a need to do something to get the positive response back.

Stats become a measuring stick for your value. A good stat line isn't just evidence of a good game — it's evidence that you matter. A poor stat line isn't just disappointment — it's a question mark over your worth. You check the box score and feel better or worse about yourself as a person based on numbers that represent maybe two or three hours of your week.

Criticism is disproportionately painful. When your coach corrects you, it shouldn't feel like an attack. A coach's correction is almost always about a play, a decision, a technique — it's professional feedback about performance. But when identity is wrapped up in performance, a coaching correction can feel like a personal rejection. It doesn't just sting — it lands somewhere deep and stays there.

Playing time becomes a referendum on your worth. Not starting doesn't just mean the coach has made a strategic lineup decision. It means something about you. Being on the bench doesn't just mean this isn't your night to play. It means maybe you don't deserve to be out there. Maybe you're not enough.

Here is what all of those experiences have in common: they take external, variable, often-arbitrary circumstances and use them to answer an internal, permanent, deeply important question.

That question is: Am I worth something?

And you're trying to answer it with playing time and stats and a coach's mood on a Tuesday afternoon. That's not a stable system. That's an emotional roller coaster with no off button, and it will exhaust you before you ever reach the ceiling of your athletic potential.

# WHY WINS FEEL SO HIGH AND LOSSES FEEL SO CRUSHING

There's a reason big wins feel almost transcendent. That feeling in the locker room after a hard-fought victory — the noise, the energy, the sense that everything went right and the work paid off — is genuinely one of the great feelings in human experience. It's not fake. It's not shallow. Competition produces real joy, real unity, real satisfaction.

But when identity is attached to performance, wins carry a freight that goes beyond athletic satisfaction. They don't just feel like a good result. They feel like confirmation. Like proof. Like a temporary answer to the question you're always quietly carrying. See? I'm good enough. See? I earned my spot. See? I matter.

The problem is that the relief of confirmation doesn't last. It wears off. And when it does, you need another win, another standout performance, another positive signal from the outside world to feel stable again. The cycle keeps running. The wins feel great, but the peace doesn't hold.

And then comes the loss.

When identity is on the line, losing is not just disappointing. It feels like a verdict. Not just that the team lost tonight, but that you lost — as a player, maybe as a person. The failure isn't just in the result. It's in you. And that version of losing follows you around for days, waking up with you in the morning, sitting across from you at the dinner table, making the next week of practice feel like you're dragging something heavy behind you that nobody else can see.

This is worth sitting with for a second, because a lot of athletes have been told to "shake it off" or "be mentally tough" without anyone ever addressing the actual source of why losses hit so hard. It's not just that you care about winning — caring about winning is fine. It's that on some level you've been using winning to answer a question that winning was never designed to answer.

The same is true for slumps. A slump should be a performance issue — a temporary dip in production that gets addressed through analysis, adjustment, and patient repetition. But when identity is on the line, a slump becomes a crisis of self. Who am I if I'm not performing well? What happens to my value if my numbers drop? What if I never get it back? Those questions have no good answer inside the performance-based framework, because in that framework, a struggling athlete is a struggling person. And that's a terrifying place to be.

*"For you created my inmost being; you knit me together in my mother's womb. I praise you because I am fearfully and wonderfully made; your works are wonderful, I know that full well." — **Psalm 139:13–14***

Read those words and notice what they are based on. Not what David accomplished. Not his stats, his wins, his battles won. But the fact that he was made — knit together by God, known from before he ever entered the world. His worth established before his first impressive act, before anyone evaluated his performance, before the outside world ever weighed in on what he was worth.

That's the foundation. Not the scoreboard.

## THE MOMENTS THAT SHAKE EVERYTHING

There are specific moments in an athlete's life that tend to be especially destabilizing when identity is tied to performance. Not just hard moments athletically, but moments that reach down into the deeper questions and pull them up to the surface where they can't be ignored.

Getting benched is one of them.

There are few experiences in competitive sport that land quite as hard as moving from starter to backup. Coaches present it as a performance-based decision — because most of the time it is. But that doesn't make it feel impersonal. Being benched feels like a demotion that goes beyond your role on the team. Especially in front of teammates you've competed alongside all season, in front of fans who have watched you start for months, in front of your parents in the stands who don't fully understand what just happened. The public nature of it adds a layer of shame that a simple conversation about a position change can't entirely address.

If your identity is rooted in your starting spot, losing that spot doesn't just change your role. It changes who you think you are. And that is an almost unbearable experience for a teenage athlete who hasn't been given the tools to separate his performance from his personhood.

Injury is another one. Injury takes everything the benching does and adds the dimension of helplessness. At least when you're benched, you can work harder, get better, and fight for your position back. When you're injured, you can't do anything. You just sit and watch. You watch someone else take your spot and start making plays in your position, and something about that particular pain — the combination of physical discomfort, lost opportunity, and the creeping fear that maybe you won't come back the same — is genuinely brutal.

Athletes who derive their entire identity from sport often find injury to be among the most psychologically difficult experiences of their lives. Without the sport, they don't quite know who they are. The structure that organized everything — the routine, the relationships, the sense of purpose, the daily affirmation of effort — is gone. And in the vacuum left behind, the questions get louder.

Being overlooked is quieter but just as corrosive. Not starting because someone else is slightly better. Not getting recruited while a teammate does. Putting in the same work, showing up every day, giving everything you have

— and watching someone else get recognized for it. Being passed over by the coaches who evaluate you. Being the one whose name doesn't get called even when you thought you'd done enough.

Overlooked athletes often internalize the oversight as evidence of their worth. I wasn't chosen because I'm not good enough. I wasn't recognized because I don't deserve recognition. The logical explanation — that sports are competitive, that multiple people can be working hard, that coaches make decisions based on many factors beyond pure effort — gets drowned out by the emotional conclusion: I wasn't enough.

All of these moments — the benching, the slump, the injury, the overlooking — are painful in their own right. But when identity is rooted in performance, they stop being hard seasons and start being identity crises. And that's a weight too heavy for any athlete to carry long-term.

*You are not your injury. You are not your slump. You are not your playing time. You never were.*

That's not empty comfort. That is the most stabilizing truth available to you in those moments. And the only way it becomes a real anchor instead of a nice-sounding phrase is if you've built your identity on something strong enough to hold before the crisis arrives.

# THE COMPARISON TRAP: THE THIEF NOBODY TALKS ABOUT

Of all the things that quietly corrode an athlete's confidence and peace, comparison might be the most pervasive and the most underestimated.

Comparison is everywhere in sports, and some of it is completely legitimate. Scouting opponents. Studying film of better players to improve your own game. Understanding where you rank in a competitive field so you know what level of work is required. That kind of comparison is just information — useful, rational, tool-like.

The comparison that damages identity is different. It's the comparison that runs automatically, constantly, and emotionally. The kind where you're not evaluating data — you're measuring your worth.

It starts small. Your teammate had a better game than you last Friday. He's getting more compliments from the coach. His social media posts about the game got more response. He's being talked about as a college prospect and your name isn't coming up in the same conversations. Another guy at your position on a different team is being recruited hard, and you've been working just as hard for just as long. A freshman comes into the program with more raw talent than you've ever had, and you start doing the math on what that means for your future role.

Each one of those things, on its own, is manageable. But comparison doesn't usually come one at a time. It comes in waves, hitting from multiple directions — teammate vs. teammate, program vs. program, your stats vs.

someone else's stats, your body type vs. someone else's, your recognition level vs. someone else's. And underneath it all, the same anxious question: How do I measure up?

When you're trying to measure your worth by comparison, there are two possible outcomes, and neither of them is actually peace. Either you come out ahead — and feel a brief relief that immediately requires re-confirmation because someone else's numbers just updated — or you come out behind, and feel the sick mixture of inadequacy and resentment that comparison almost always produces.

That second feeling — the inadequacy and resentment blend — is one of the more uncomfortable emotional places an athlete can occupy, partly because it doesn't feel admirable to be there. Most athletes are taught to be good team-mates. They know they're supposed to be happy for the guy who's getting more playing time, who's getting more attention, who's being recruited more heavily. And on some level they are happy for him. But there's also something painful running underneath the genuine support, something they're not sure they're allowed to acknowledge, a question that makes them feel small for even having it: Why him and not me?

Comparison never answers that question satisfactorily. Because comparison operates on the assumption that there is a fixed amount of worth available, and whoever is doing better than you is somehow taking what could have been yours. That's a scarcity mindset, and it is exhausting to live inside.

*"For we dare not make ourselves of the number, or compare ourselves with some that commend themselves: but they measuring themselves by themselves, and comparing themselves among themselves, are not wise."* — **2 Corinthians 10:12 (KJV)**

Paul's assessment is direct: comparison as a measurement of worth is not wise. Not because it's immoral, but because it's structurally flawed. It can't give you what you're looking for. Measuring your worth by comparison to other people puts your sense of value entirely at the mercy of their performance — a moving target you cannot control and will never definitively beat, because there will always be someone ahead of you in some category if you look hard enough.

The only comparison that actually helps is the one you do with your own past self. Are you improving? Are you more disciplined than you were six months ago? Are you a better teammate, a harder worker, a more mentally mature athlete than you used to be? That comparison is useful. That comparison actually builds something.

## THE UNSTABLE FOUNDATION

Here is a truth that nobody tells teenage athletes, and that most of them have to learn the hard way: sports will eventually fail you as an identity.

Not because sports are bad. Not because your athletic career doesn't matter. But because the nature of sports — the seasonal, variable, competitive, physically demanding, externally evaluated nature of sports — makes it a fundamentally unstable foundation for the deepest questions of who you are.

Consider the variability alone. Your performance fluctuates. Some games you're on, some games you're off. Some seasons you're healthy, some you're not. Some years the team around you is strong, some years it isn't. Your role changes as you age and as new players come in. Your relationship with coaches changes. The sport's demands on your body change as you move through different levels of competition. Nothing in the athletic landscape stays the same long enough to serve as a stable definition of who you are.

And then there's the ceiling. At some point, every athletic career ends. For some guys that's at eighteen. For some it's at twenty-two. For the very rare, very gifted few, it extends into professional sport — but even then, it ends. The average professional sports career across most major sports is somewhere between three and six years. The athletes who built their entire identity on their sport often describe retirement as one of the most disorienting experiences of their lives. Not just because they miss competing — though they do — but because they don't know who they are without it. The thing that answered the identity question for all those years just... stopped.

You don't have to wait until your playing days are over to start building an identity that holds. You can start now. And if you do it now, you'll actually play better in the meantime — because a secure identity competes differently than an insecure one.

The simplest way to evaluate whether your identity is well-founded is to ask: if you were told tomorrow that you could never play your sport again, who would you be? What would be left? If the honest answer is "I'm not sure" or "I don't know how I'd handle that" — that's not a character flaw. That's a signal. And signals are meant to redirect you somewhere better.

*If your sport disappeared tomorrow, everything that actually matters about you would still be there. The question is whether you know that.*

You are a son. A friend. A human being made with particular gifts, a particular personality, a particular history, and a particular future that no stat line can summarize. You have a sense of humor, a way of thinking, a capacity for loyalty and courage and compassion that exists completely independently of how well you performed last Saturday. You are known by a God who knew you before you ever picked up a ball, put on a uniform, or laced up a pair of cleats.

That is not nothing. That is everything.

# WHAT IDENTITY IN CHRIST ACTUALLY MEANS FOR AN ATHLETE

When people in church circles talk about "identity in Christ," it can sound vague and abstract in a way that doesn't immediately connect to the concrete reality of athletic life. So let's make it specific.

Identity in Christ means that the most foundational truth about who you are is established by God — not by your performance, not by other people's opinions, not by your stats or your role or your record. It means that the question "am I worth something?" has already been answered, at the highest possible level, in a way that nothing you do or fail to do can change.

The answer to that question was given at the cross. God, who is not impressed by talent or moved by highlight reels, who does not evaluate worth by athletic metrics, demonstrated the full weight of how He values you before you ever proved yourself to anyone. While you were still flawed, still failing, still nowhere near your best version — He made the ultimate move. That's how much you're worth. Not what you deserve when you perform well. What He determined before you had the chance to perform at all.

1 John 3:1 puts it in a way that is almost too simple to take seriously until you let it actually land: See what great love the Father has lavished on us, that we should be called children of God! And that is what we are.

Children of God. That's your identity. Not athlete. Not starter or backup. Not standout prospect or overlooked role player. Not the guy who had a great season or the guy who struggled. Child of God. That identity was given, not earned. It cannot be taken by a bad game, a lost position, an injury, or a coach who stopped believing in you.

What this means practically for an athlete is significant. It means you can walk into the biggest game of your life with your identity already settled. The outcome of the game is not going to change who you are. The question of your worth is not on the table today. You are not out there trying to earn something you don't have. You already have it. You're playing from that place, not toward it.

It means that when a bad game happens — and bad games will happen, this is not a theology that prevents difficulty — it does not reach the deepest level of who you are. It stays in the category of athletic performance: frustrating, worth learning from, worth addressing, but not a verdict. Not a definition.

It means that when a teammate seems to be more talented, more recognized, more recruited, his success does not diminish your worth. Your value is not a competitive resource that gets divided up among the roster. It's not like there's only so much worth to go around and whoever performs best gets the bigger share. Each person on that team has full, complete, non-negotiable worth in the eyes of God. His success doesn't take anything from yours.

*"But now, this is what the Lord says — he who created you, Jacob, he who formed*

*you, Israel: Do not fear, for I have redeemed you; I have summoned you by name; you are mine." — **Isaiah 43:1***

Summoned by name. Known. Claimed. Before the season started. Before the recruiting evaluation. Before the coach made his lineup decisions. Before the scoreboard reflected anything about your performance.

You are mine. That's the foundation. And it doesn't move.

# PLAYING FROM IDENTITY INSTEAD OF FOR IT

This concept might be the single most important mental shift available to a competing athlete. And it's simple enough to say in one sentence, but deep enough to spend a lifetime practicing.

Playing for identity means competing in order to establish, confirm, or defend your worth. Every game is an audition. Every play is evidence you're using to build a case for your own value. Every mistake is a crack in the argument. The pressure is enormous because the stakes are existential — you're not just trying to win a game, you're trying to prove something about yourself that you're not sure is already true.

Playing from identity means competing from a foundation that is already settled. Your worth is already established. The game is not where you go to get it — the game is where you go to express it. To give what you have. To serve your team with the ability that has been placed in you. To honor God with your effort and your attitude. To compete with the fullness of who you are, with nothing held back, because the worst possible outcome of today's game cannot take away anything that actually matters.

The difference between those two athletes is visible in how they play. The athlete playing for identity tightens under pressure. He plays cautiously in big moments because mistakes are too costly to absorb. He celebrates good plays with relief as much as joy. He deflects criticism instead of receiving it, because criticism confirms what he's afraid is true. He resents the success of teammates who are also competing for a limited supply of the approval he needs. He burns hot and burns out, because the fuel he's running on — external validation — can never be reliably supplied.

The athlete playing from identity moves differently. He plays free. He takes risks because he's not protecting something fragile. He absorbs criticism as information rather than injury. He celebrates teammates' success genuinely because their wins don't diminish his worth. He competes hard in big moments because he has nothing to lose at the fundamental level. He plays with a kind of joyful intensity — fully committed, fully present, not distracted by the weight of having to prove himself.

That athlete is more fun to coach. More valuable to his team. More resilient through hard stretches. More capable of actual long-term growth. And he's happier — not in a shallow, nothing-bothers-me way, but in a deeper way that holds up even when the game doesn't go his direction.

Colossians 3:23 says: Whatever you do, work at it with all your heart, as working for the Lord, not for human masters. The theological statement there is enormous when you apply it to athletic competition. Work at it with all your heart — full effort, full intensity, nothing held back. But work as for the Lord, not for human masters. Not for the coach's approval. Not for the crowd's response. Not for the stat line or the recruiting profile or the social media response. For something bigger, something more stable, something that doesn't fluctuate with the scoreboard.

That's what competing from identity looks like in biblical terms. Full commitment. Full effort. Purpose-driven rather than approval-driven. Free from the need to perform for an audience that can never give you what you're actually looking for.

## CARING DEEPLY WITHOUT BEING OWNED

Let me be very clear about something, because this chapter could easily be misread in a way that would actually harm your athletic development.

Nothing in this chapter is telling you not to care about sports. Not to care about winning. Not to care about your performance, your improvement, your stats, your role, your team. Caring about those things is not the problem. The deep drive to compete, to improve, to win, to be excellent — that is one of the best things about you as an athlete, and nothing in this chapter should touch it.

The problem is not caring. The problem is worshiping. The problem is when sports shift from something that matters to the thing that defines you. When the game becomes your god — the source of your worth, the final arbiter of your value, the lens through which you understand everything about yourself — it will eventually do what false gods always do: fail to deliver what it promised, and cost you more than you were prepared to pay.

Caring and worshiping are different postures. The athlete who cares gives everything in practice and on game day, grieves real losses, celebrates real wins, and then releases the outcome without losing his footing. The athlete who worships can't release the outcome because releasing it means releasing the verdict on who he is. The score stays with him, the mistake loops in his head, the benching becomes a referendum on his worth, the slump becomes a crisis of identity.

You can work harder than anyone, want to win more than anyone, sacrifice more for your sport than anyone around you — and still hold it in its proper place. That's not lukewarm commitment. That's healthy commitment. It's the kind of commitment that actually sustains itself long-term, because it's not running on the volatile fuel of approval and external validation. It's running on something deeper: the joy of the craft, the love of the competition, the desire to serve your team, and the purpose of glorifying God with the ability He gave you.

There is a version of athletic excellence that is free. Fully invested, fully competitive, fully driven — and yet free from the need to have its worth confirmed by the outcome. That version is available to you. But you can't get there by caring less. You get there by finding your worth somewhere that doesn't require you to keep performing to maintain it.

# YOUR SPORT IS A GIFT. DON'T MAKE IT A GOD.

Here is a healthier frame for what sports can be — and genuinely are, when held in the right place.

Sports are a training ground for the rest of your life. The discipline you build in the weight room transfers into every area that requires sustained effort — school, work, relationships, faith. The ability to function under pressure that you're developing right now will serve you in the boardroom, the operating room, the negotiating table, the hard conversations that adult life requires. You are being prepared for things you haven't faced yet by the very sport that feels like it's just a game.

Sports are a character crucible. The moments that test you most — the losses, the setbacks, the pressure, the adversity — are the moments where character is formed. You cannot manufacture courage without something to be afraid of. You cannot develop resilience without facing difficulty. You cannot build humility without being regularly reminded that you are not in control of everything. Sports deliver those experiences with consistency and intensity, and if you're paying attention, they are building something in you that outlasts any trophy.

Sports are a platform for leadership and influence. How you carry yourself in competition — how you respond to adversity, how you treat officials, how you support a teammate who is struggling, how you handle winning and losing — is observed by more people than you realize. Younger athletes on your team are watching you. Your community is watching. How you play says something about what you believe. Playing with integrity, with grace, with genuine competitive fire and genuine respect for the people around you — that is a form of witness that goes further than a lot of conversations ever could.

Sports can be an act of worship. Not in a performance-for-God kind of way, where you dedicate your stats to Him and hope He appreciates the numbers. But in the way that 1 Corinthians 10:31 frames it: whether you eat or drink or whatever you do, do it all for the glory of God. Giving your genuine best effort. Competing with the full use of the ability He placed in you. Refusing to mail it in when things get hard. Playing with integrity. These are not just athletic virtues — they are forms of honoring the One who made you and gave you those gifts.

Sports are a gift. A genuinely great gift. Physical ability is not something you manufactured — it was given to you, and the opportunity to develop it, compete with it, and share it with a team is something not everyone gets. Holding that awareness — that gratitude — does something to how you compete. Gratitude competes differently than entitlement. Gratitude plays free. Entitlement plays tight and angry.

None of that is true of a god. Gods demand. Gods consume. Gods require constant sacrifice and return nothing that is permanent. When sports become a god, they take the joy out of the very thing you love, because every game becomes a transaction — performance in exchange for worth — rather than an expression of genuine human excellence and the God-given capacity for competition.

Hold it well. Give it everything. Compete with your whole heart. And know that your whole heart was never meant to be owned by the outcome.

## THE FOUNDATION THAT HOLDS

The next time you're in that car after a bad game, and the silence is heavy, and the replay is running, and the feeling that's sitting in your chest feels bigger than just disappointment —

Remember this.

The feeling is real. The game mattered. The disappointment is legitimate. You're allowed to feel it. But it is not a verdict. It is not a summary of your worth. It is a hard moment in a season, in a journey, in a life that is already more valuable than any single result can measure.

You are more than your last game. You were more before you ever played one.

Your identity is not on the scoreboard. It's not in the stat column. It's not in the coach's evaluation, the recruiting ranking, the starting lineup, or the postgame reaction of the people in the stands. It is in the unchanging declaration of the God who made you: I have summoned you by name. You are mine.

That foundation does not crack under a bad performance. It does not shift when the coach makes a decision that didn't go your way. It does not erode through a slump or an injury or a season that didn't go the way you planned. It holds because it was never built on the things that change. It was built on the One who doesn't.

Go back and compete with everything you have. Chase excellence. Work harder than you've worked. Want to win with your whole competitive heart. Play with full intensity, full effort, full presence.

But play free. Because the question of your worth? That one's already been answered.

And the answer has nothing to do with the scoreboard.

## A PRAYER FOR THIS MOMENT

*God, I want to be honest about something: I've been letting sports answer a question*

*You were supposed to answer. My confidence has been rising and falling with my performance, and that's exhausting. I'm tired of living that way.*

*Help me to really believe — not just know in my head, but feel and live — that my worth is settled. That I'm yours. That You knew me before any of this, and You'll still know me the same way regardless of how this season goes.*

*Take back the part of my identity that I've handed to sports. I want to compete hard and care deeply, but I don't want the game to own me.*

*Teach me to play from the foundation You've given me, not toward a foundation I'm trying to build with my performance. Help me to compete free.*

*And on the bad days — the benched days, the slump days, the quiet car ride home days — remind me who I am before You. That's enough. Amen.*

## THINK ON THIS

1. When did you first start connecting how you play with how you feel about yourself as a person? Can you remember a specific moment when the two got tangled together?

2. What specific circumstance most threatens your identity right now — playing time, comparison, a slump, someone else's success? What does that tell you about where you're looking for worth?

3. What would be different about how you compete if you genuinely believed your worth was already settled before the game started?

4. What has your sport taught you about yourself — not as an athlete, but as a person? What character qualities have been built through competing?

## GAME-DAY CHALLENGE

This week, try this identity reset exercise:

Write down three things that are true about you that have absolutely nothing to do with sports. Not your athletic accomplishments — the things about who you are as a person. Your character. The way you show up for people. What you care about. What makes you, you.

Keep that list somewhere you can see it.

Then, before your next game or practice, read it. Not as a ritual, but as a reminder. You are showing up today as a person who already has worth — and you're about to go express some of it on the field.

Notice if anything shifts in how you feel walking in.

# CHAPTER 3
# NEXT PLAY

BOUNCING BACK AFTER MISTAKES, *Losses, and Bad Games*

*"The righteous man falls seven times, and rises again."* — **Proverbs 24:16**

## THE MOMENT EVERYTHING GOES WRONG

You already know the feeling before you can even fully describe it.

It might be the dropped pass in the end zone — the one that hit you right in the hands and bounced away while the whole stadium either went silent or groaned. It might be the free throw in the final minute of a close game, two easy shots that you've made ten thousand times in practice, except this time one of them clanked off the back rim and the other one didn't even draw iron. It might be the turnover — a pass you telegraphed, a ball you coughed up, a decision your brain made half a second too late. It might be the missed tackle on a runner who went on to score. The strikeout with runners on base and the game tied. The blown assignment that gave the defense an easy look. The serve that sailed long when you needed it in.

The moment itself lasts maybe two seconds.

What happens next can last a lot longer.

In the immediate aftermath of a mistake, something fires in a competing athlete that is very hard to describe to someone who has never experienced it. It's not just embarrassment, though that's part of it. It's not just frustration, though that's there too. It's this specific, acute cocktail of emotion that mixes shame and anger and exposure and the sudden desperate wish that you could rewind the last three seconds of your life. Your face heats up. Your jaw tightens. Your teammates are looking at you, or maybe they're carefully not looking at you, and somehow both of those feel equally bad.

And then — here is where the real damage can happen — your brain starts running.

The game is still going. The clock is still ticking, the ball is still live, the next possession is already starting. But part of your mind is no longer present. It's back at the mistake, replaying it from every angle, analyzing it, prosecuting it. You're still in your body on the court or field, going through the physical motions. But your focus, your presence, your mental edge — they're stuck two plays back.

That is the real cost of a mistake badly handled. Not the mistake itself. The aftermath.

Because here is the thing every honest athlete eventually has to reckon with: one bad play almost never ends a game. But a bad mental response to one bad play absolutely can. The spiral from a single mistake into a bad half, a bad game, a bad week — that happens all the time. And it happens not because the athlete lacked talent, but because he lacked the tools to reset.

This chapter is about building those tools.

## WHY MISTAKES HIT HARDER THAN THEY SHOULD

If mistakes were just mistakes — isolated events with no emotional freight, just data points in a performance review — athletes would process them quickly and move on. But that is almost never how it actually works. Most athletes, especially young ones, carry a disproportionate emotional response to their own errors. The mistake feels bigger than it is. The pain lasts longer than it should. And understanding why is the first step toward changing it.

Part of it is simply the high-stakes environment of competition. When you care deeply about something and you are being evaluated in real time in front of coaches, teammates, opponents, and spectators, your brain processes mistakes as social threats. Human beings are wired to be deeply sensitive to social evaluation — to what others think of us and how we appear in the eyes of our group. In prehistoric terms, being seen as incompetent or unreliable by your tribe was genuinely dangerous. Evolution didn't update that wiring just because the stakes are now a basketball game instead of a mammoth hunt.

So when you drop the ball in a critical moment, your nervous system treats it with a level of urgency that is somewhat out of proportion to the actual situation. Your heart rate spikes. Your thoughts narrow. The mistake gets amplified in your perception — it feels more visible, more significant, more defining than it probably is to anyone who actually watched it happen.

Part of it, as Chapter 2 covered, is identity. When performance is the foundation of your worth, a performance failure is a threat to something much more important than your stat line. It feels personal because, in the framework your brain has been quietly operating in, it is personal. The dropped pass isn't just a bad play — it's evidence. Evidence you're not good enough. Evidence your spot on the depth chart is less secure than you thought. Evidence that the people who believed in you might be wrong to do so.

And part of it is perfectionism, which is one of the most common and least examined traits in competitive athletes. Perfectionism sounds like a virtue — the relentless pursuit of excellence, the refusal to settle for anything less than your best. And in some forms, the drive for excellence is genuinely valuable. But perfectionism in its unhealthy form is not a high standard. It's a belief that mistakes are unacceptable, that errors reveal something shameful about who you are, that anything short of perfect is a kind of failure. That belief makes every mistake feel catastrophic, every criticism feel like condemnation, and every normal human limitation feel like a character flaw.

Perfectionist athletes often work incredibly hard. They're often among the most committed people in the room. But they're also usually the ones who are hardest on themselves, who struggle most to reset after mistakes, and who carry the heaviest emotional load through a long season.

## PERFECTIONISM IS NOT A HIGH STANDARD. IT'S FEAR WEARING THE COSTUME OF EXCELLENCE.

There is a difference between the pursuit of excellence — working hard, caring about quality, pushing yourself to improve — and perfectionism, which demands that you never fail and responds to failure with shame. The first builds athletes. The second slowly breaks them down.

Understanding why your mistakes hit as hard as they do is not an exercise in making excuses. It's an exercise in self-awareness. You can't change a pattern you haven't named. And the first step toward a better response to failure is recognizing what's actually happening when the mistake hits and the spiral starts.

## HOW ONE BAD PLAY BECOMES A BAD GAME

Let's walk through the spiral in real time, because it has a recognizable shape and most athletes will see themselves in it immediately.

It starts with the mistake. Let's say it's a turnover — a pass intercepted in the third quarter of a close game. The immediate reaction is a flash of frustration. Fine. Normal. That's just honest emotion.

But then the internal monologue starts. Why did I do that? That was so stupid. Coach is going to pull me. Everyone saw that. We were right there and I just gave it away. I can't believe I threw that.

Notice what's happening. The event is already over. The other team has the ball. The game is still being played. But your attention is no longer on the game — it's on the mistake and on the story you're building around it.

Your body follows your mind. The shoulders drop slightly. The jaw stays tight. The movements become a little stiffer, a little more cautious. You're no longer competing freely — you're protecting yourself from making another mistake, which means you're now operating from fear instead of instinct.

The next play, you have a chance to redeem yourself. A pass comes your way and something in you wants to force it — to make the big play, to prove the last one didn't define you, to quiet the voice in your head and the looks from the sideline. So instead of making the right read, you force something that isn't quite there. Another mistake. Now the spiral tightens.

Or the opposite happens: the pass comes your way and you hesitate. You don't want to make another mistake. You hold it a half-second too long, and the window closes. Incomplete. Another wasted opportunity.

Either way, the mistake in the third quarter has now contaminated the fourth quarter. One bad play has become a bad game, not because your talent disappeared, not because the situation demanded more than you were capable of, but because your mental response to the mistake pulled you out of the present moment and put you in a loop you couldn't escape.

This is not theoretical. This happens in almost every sport, at every level, to athletes of every talent level. The difference between the athletes who recover from mistakes quickly and the ones who spiral is almost never about talent. It's about the speed and effectiveness of their mental reset.

*"Do not be anxious about anything, but in every situation, by prayer and petition, with thanksgiving, present your requests to God. And the peace of God, which transcends all understanding, will guard your hearts and your minds in Christ Jesus." — **Philippians 4:6–7**

Notice the phrase that is easy to read past: guard your hearts and your minds. Not just your feelings — your minds. The peace of God actively protects your thinking from being hijacked by the spiral of anxiety. That protection is available in the middle of a game, not just after it. But accessing it requires a practice — the practice of bringing your mind back to what is true when the spiral starts pulling it somewhere else.

That is the biblical next-play mindset. And it is learnable.

## WHY SOME ATHLETES STAY STUCK

If resetting after mistakes is so important, why is it so hard? Why do so many athletes — talented, hard-working, genuinely competitive athletes — keep getting pulled back into the spiral instead of escaping it?

The first reason is that nobody taught them how. This sounds almost too simple, but it's true. Mental recovery after mistakes is a skill, and most athletic development programs put enormous time into physical skills and almost none into the mental recovery skills that determine how athletes perform over the course of a game and a season. You've had coaches teach you footwork, ball skills, strength, conditioning, strategy. Has anyone ever sat down with you and walked you through what to do in the thirty seconds after a mistake? How to reset your body language? How to redirect your attention? How to replace the spiral thought with a functional one?

For most athletes, the answer is no. You've been told to shake it off, but nobody explained how shaking it off actually works.

The second reason is pride. This is worth being honest about. Pride — the defensive, self-protecting kind — can make it very difficult to process a mistake cleanly. Because processing a mistake cleanly requires a brief moment of genuine acknowledgment: I made that error. That was on me. That's a harder admission than it sounds for an athlete who has spent years defining himself by his competence. Admitting a mistake honestly, without deflection, requires the kind of humility that feels like exposure. Pride would rather stay angry than become vulnerable, even for a second. Pride would rather blame the conditions, the officiating, the teammate who should have been in a different position — anything to avoid the clean, honest acknowledgment that frees you to move on.

The third reason is shame. Shame and guilt are different in an important way. Guilt says: I did something wrong. Shame says: I am something wrong. Guilt can motivate change. Shame just immobilizes. When an athlete responds to a mistake with shame rather than guilt, they don't process it and grow from it — they get buried by it. The mistake becomes evidence of a deeper inadequacy, and the emotional weight of that evidence is too heavy to carry into the next play productively.

Shame thrives in performance-based identity, because in that framework, a performance failure is always a personal failure. But when identity is rooted in something more stable than performance, mistakes lose their power to generate shame. They remain disappointing, worth learning from, worth addressing — but not shattering.

The fourth reason is rehearsal. Most athletes, after a bad play, replay it. They replay it on the bench, they replay it in the locker room, they replay it on the way home, they replay it before they fall asleep. Neurologically, every time you replay a memory in vivid detail, you strengthen the neural pathway associated with it. In other words: the more you relive the mistake, the more deeply it gets encoded. The more deeply it gets encoded, the more easily it gets triggered in future similar situations. You are, quite literally, training yourself to make the same mistake under pressure by spending hours replaying it without the context of learning and moving forward.

Reviewing a mistake once, specifically, with the intention of understanding what happened and what to do differently — that's valuable. That's learning. But replaying it emotionally and repeatedly, without any corrective framework? That's just making it worse.

## LOSING WITHOUT LOSING YOURSELF

Mistakes happen during games. But what about the whole thing — when the game itself is a loss? When the final whistle blows and the scoreboard says you didn't get it done? When all the effort and preparation and sacrifice of the season ran directly into a team that was better on this particular day?

Loss is one of the most honest teachers in human experience. It shows up uninvited, strips away everything comfortable, and leaves you with nothing but reality and questions. And the questions it raises are often significant ones: How do I respond to this? What does this say about where I am? What do I do now?

For the athlete whose identity is secure, those questions have answers that hold. I respond to this with honest disappointment and renewed resolve. This says I faced something hard and it hurt and that's okay. I go back to work. For the athlete whose identity is fragile, those questions become much more destabilizing: Am I good enough? Was all that effort for nothing? What do people think of me right now?

Here's what a loss can legitimately be, and what it cannot.

A loss can be genuinely disappointing. You worked hard, you competed, and you didn't get the result you wanted. That is a real disappointment, and there is no spiritual maturity in pretending it isn't. Great competitors feel loss deeply. They feel it because they care, and caring is not the problem.

A loss can reveal things that need to improve. Maybe there were breakdowns in execution, in preparation, in decision-making under pressure. Loss has information in it, and the athletes who mine that information carefully are the ones who grow from defeat into something better.

A loss can build character. Resilience doesn't grow in the absence of adversity. The young man who learns how to pick himself back up after a genuine defeat — not just pretend to shake it off, but actually process it and come back with renewed purpose — is developing something that will serve him for the rest of his life.

What a loss cannot legitimately be is the final word on your worth. It cannot be a verdict on your future. It cannot be evidence that your effort was meaningless or that your potential is limited. One game, one season, one disappointing result does not get to write the summary of who you are. That's not denial — it's just an accurate reading of what a loss actually is and isn't.

## EVERY GREAT ATHLETE IN HISTORY HAS A LOSS ON THEIR RECORD. MOST OF THEM HAVE A LOT.

*The ones who became great decided what those losses meant.*

Carrying a loss into Monday's practice as motivation is healthy. Carrying it into Monday's practice as shame is not. The first version learns from the defeat and comes back sharper. The second version comes back heavier and more afraid of the next loss — which, ironically, makes the next loss more likely.

After a big loss, your job is simple. Grieve it briefly and honestly. Feel the disappointment. Don't stuff it. Then decide: what's actually in my control from here? What did I learn? What do I go back and address? And who am I, regardless of the scoreboard?

Answer that last question right, and no loss gets to own you.

## GRACE: WHAT IT ACTUALLY DOES FOR A COMPETING ATHLETE

The word grace gets used a lot in Christian circles, sometimes in ways that are so broad they lose their practical meaning. So let's get specific about what grace actually does for an athlete who just had the worst game of his season.

Grace does not mean that your mistakes don't matter. They do. If you threw the interception, the interception happened. If you missed the assignment, the defense gave up the score. If you came off the bench and played poorly, the team was worse for it in that stretch. Grace doesn't erase consequences. Real life doesn't have a delete button, and a healthy theology of grace doesn't pretend it does.

Grace does not mean accountability is optional. You still have to look your coach in the eye. You still have to own your mistakes in a film session. You still have to put in the work to correct what went wrong. Grace is not a free pass from responsibility. It's not an excuse to stop caring about excellence.

What grace does — and this is enormous if you actually let it land — is separate your performance from your verdict.

In a merit-based system, failure has a direct cost to your standing. You mess up, you lose points. Your record gets marked. You're worth less in the eyes of the one judging you. That's how the world tends to operate, and it's the logic that makes bad games feel so unbearable — because in performance-based thinking, the logic of the world is the logic you're living under.

Grace operates on entirely different logic. Grace says: you failed, and your standing with God is unchanged. You threw the worst game of your life, and you are no less His. You are no less loved, no less known, no less called by name. The failure happened. It doesn't define you. It doesn't determine your value. It doesn't separate you from anything that actually matters.

That is not a small thing. That is a foundation that can hold through the worst game, the worst season, the worst moment of your athletic career. Because the worst moment of your athletic career, in the framework of grace, is still not the final word on who you are.

*"He gives strength to the weary and increases the power of the weak. Even youths grow tired and weary, and young men stumble and fall; but those who hope in the Lord will renew their strength. They will soar on wings like eagles; they will run and not grow weary, they will walk and not be faint." — Isaiah 40:29–31*

The imagery here is worth sitting with. Even youths grow tired and weary. Even young men stumble and fall. Isaiah is not describing the weak or the faithless here — he is describing you. The young, the capable, the energetic athlete. Even that person stumbles. The stumbling is assumed. It is part of the story, not the end of it.

But those who hope in the Lord will renew their strength. The reset is available. The restoration is real. The capacity to go again — after the mistake, after the loss, after the slump — is not something you generate from within your own willpower. It's something that comes from something stronger than you.

That is the theological foundation of the next-play mindset. You don't reset through sheer mental toughness alone. You reset through a genuine trust in the One who is already past your mistake, already in your next play, already working in your weakness in ways you can't fully see yet.

## THE NEXT-PLAY MINDSET: WHAT IT ACTUALLY LOOKS LIKE

"Next play" is a phrase coaches use all the time, and it's genuinely good coaching. But like a lot of good coaching phrases, it's more often stated than explained. So let's actually break down what a next-play mindset looks like in practice — not as a bumper sticker, but as a real mental process you can use in real time.

Step one is acknowledgment. Not denial, not deflection, not immediate suppression — acknowledgment. You made the mistake. You know it. You own it, quickly and honestly, in a single internal moment. Yes, that happened. That was on me. This is not self-destruction. This is not a spiral. It's a clean, honest, two-second recognition of reality. I dropped the ball. I missed the shot. I made the wrong call.

The acknowledgment step is important because the alternative — denial and deflection — actually prolongs the problem. Athletes who can't honestly acknowledge their mistakes spend enormous mental energy protecting themselves from the admission, which ironically keeps the mistake in focus longer. The clean acknowledgment clears the slate to move forward.

Step two is release. Once you've acknowledged it, you release it from your active attention. Not because it doesn't matter. Not because you'll never think about it again. But because right now, in this moment, the game is still happening. The clock hasn't stopped. Your team still needs you present. You can process this fully after — after the game, after the emotions have settled, after you've had time to think clearly. Right now, the release is: that play is over. I'm bringing myself back to now.

A lot of athletes find a physical anchor helpful for this release. A deep breath, a shake of the hands, a quick tap of the chest — some small physical gesture that your body learns to associate with the mental act of resetting. Athletes from Michael Jordan to countless Olympians have talked about the importance of a reset ritual. It's not superstition. It's neuroscience: creating a physical cue that triggers a mental state you've practiced.

Step three is redirect. After releasing, you bring your attention forward — specifically to the next job. Not the general idea of "doing better." The next specific assignment. On defense, your assignment right now is this man. In the box, this at-bat is only about this pitch. On the line, this snap is a clean slate. The redirect is precise and present-focused.

Step four — and this is where faith enters in a practical way — is a word of truth. Not a speech. Not a long internal pep talk. A single grounding truth, spoken quickly to yourself, that reconnects you to a foundation bigger than the mistake. Something like: My identity is not in this play. Or: God is with me right now. Or simply: Next play. Said with intention, not as desperation, but as an act of choosing what you're going to stand on in this moment.

The whole process — acknowledge, release, redirect, truth — can happen in under thirty seconds. Most of the time it happens in under ten. It is not a luxury available only in slow-paced sports or during timeouts. It is a rapid internal sequence that, with practice, becomes automatic. Like any other skill, it feels slow and deliberate at first, and eventually becomes fluid and instinctive.

## THE NEXT PLAY IS ALWAYS A CLEAN SLATE.

*You only make it dirty by dragging the last one into it.*

That's not inspirational fiction. That is how high performers in every demanding field — sports, military operations, surgery, high-stakes negotiation — are trained to think. The present moment is always recoverable. The only thing that makes it unrecoverable is the decision to import the last moment's failure into it.

## PRACTICAL RECOVERY TOOLS: REAL THINGS YOU CAN ACTUALLY USE

Beyond the next-play process, here are a set of specific tools that help athletes recover faster after mistakes. These are not abstract principles. They are concrete practices that translate directly into game situations.

Reset your body language intentionally.

Your body communicates to your brain just as much as your brain communicates to your body. Research consistently shows that adopting open, upright, confident physical posture actually influences your mental and emotional state — not just the other way around. After a mistake, the instinctive response is to hunch, to look down, to physically contract. That body language reinforces the negative mental state. Doing the opposite — consciously squaring your shoulders, lifting your chin, walking with purpose — actually begins to interrupt the spiral at the physiological level. It sounds almost too simple. Try it and see what happens.

Replace the repeat replay with a single specific review.

After the game is over and the emotions have settled — not in the middle of competition — allow yourself one clear, analytical review of the mistake. What happened? Why? What would I do differently? Get specific, get honest, then close the file. The goal is information, not self-punishment. One clear review gives you something to work on. Twenty emotional replays give you anxiety and a worse night's sleep.

Use short reset prayers.

This doesn't have to be a thirty-second theological exercise in the middle of a possession. It can be as short as a single honest phrase: God, reset me. Or: Help me be present. Or simply: I trust you with this. That brief, intentional act of turning your attention toward God — even for a few seconds — does something to the spiral. It interrupts it with a different reference point. Instead of your mind looping on the mistake and what it might mean about you, you're briefly anchoring to the One for whom the mistake is not a surprise, not a catastrophe, and not the end of the story.

Focus on your next specific job, not your general performance.

"Do better" is not a useful instruction. It's too broad, too vague, and too focused on outcome rather than process. After a mistake, the redirect should be specific: my job right now is to communicate this screen. My job right now is to get my feet set before catching the next ball. My job right now is to attack the first pitch. The more specific and process-oriented the redirect, the more effectively it breaks the outcome-anxiety loop.

Give yourself the same grace you'd give a teammate.

This is one of the most revealing tests available. If your teammate made the same mistake you just made, what would you say to him? Probably something like: Shake it off. Next play. We're still in this. You might put a hand on his shoulder. You'd encourage him to reset and get back in it. You would almost certainly not say the things to him that you're saying to yourself right now.

There is something important in that discrepancy. It reveals that the standard you're holding yourself to is harsher than the one you'd apply to anyone else you care about. That asymmetry is not righteous — it's just unkind. And it's unkind toward someone who has done a lot of work and who deserves the same compassion he would freely offer a struggling teammate.

Applying grace to yourself is not weakness. It is wisdom. It is the practice of treating yourself as someone who is known and loved by God — which means extending to yourself something of the mercy that God extends freely.

## SLUMPS, SETBACKS, AND SEASONS THAT WON'T TURN

Everything we've discussed so far has been about single mistakes and single losses. But what about when it keeps happening? What about the slump that stretches from one game to three games to two months? What about the season where nothing goes right, where every week brings another disappointment, where the work doesn't seem to translate into results, where you're starting to quietly wonder if you've lost something that might not come back?

Slumps are a specific kind of hard. They have a different emotional texture than a single bad game. A bad game ends. A slump doesn't know when it's over, which means every game during a slump carries the additional anxiety of wondering: is this the one where it comes back? And when it doesn't come back today, the worry deepens. Maybe it's not a slump. Maybe this is just what I am now.

That thought — maybe this is just what I am now — is one of the more psychologically corrosive thoughts an athlete can have. It takes what is almost certainly a temporary performance dip and recasts it as a permanent verdict on ability and potential. And once you start believing that thought, the anxiety it generates actually makes the slump worse, which generates more evidence for the thought, which deepens the anxiety. It becomes a feedback loop with no obvious exit.

Getting out of that loop requires separating performance from identity — again, and more deliberately than usual, because the accumulation of hard results makes the separation much harder to maintain. It requires reminding yourself, repeatedly and with some real effort, that a slump is a performance pattern, not a character summary. That you are not your shooting percentage right now. That your work has meaning even when the results aren't reflecting it yet.

It also requires patience, which is perhaps the most counter-cultural athletic virtue available. Athletes are trained to respond with urgency. Work harder, adjust faster, fix it now. And some of that is right and necessary. But patience — the willingness to keep doing the right things even when they're not producing immediate results, to trust the process even when the process feels stuck — is something that a slump specifically demands.

*"And we know that in all things God works for the good of those who love him, who have been called according to his purpose." — **Romans 8:28***

All things. Not the winning things, not the comfortable things, not the spiritually convenient things. All things. The slump. The hard season. The month where nothing went right. God is working in those things — not despite the difficulty but through it. Not to punish you or to signal that He's finished with you, but because the formation that happens in difficulty cannot happen in comfort.

That doesn't make the slump feel better in the moment. But it changes what the slump means. It isn't abandoned time. It isn't wasted. Something is being built in you during this stretch that might not be visible yet, but it's real. The question is not whether God is doing something in your hard season. The question is whether you're paying attention to what it is.

Many of the best athletes have a hard season in their history — a stretch of time that, from the inside, felt like it might be the end of something, but from the outside (or in retrospect) was clearly the beginning of something better. The slump that forced them to rebuild their mechanics. The hard year that stripped away the superficial confidence and built something more durable underneath. The setback that redirected them toward an approach they never would have found otherwise.

You may be in that stretch right now. You may be in the part of the story that doesn't feel like a story yet — it just feels like difficulty with no obvious resolution. If so: stay in it. Do the work. Trust the process more deeply than the results. Keep showing up with the best you have, and keep bringing the weight of it to God instead of trying to carry it alone.

## WHAT FAILURE TEACHES THAT SUCCESS NEVER WILL

Let's say something honest about failure that nobody really wants to hear: some of the most important things you will ever learn as a competitor and as a person will come through losing, not winning.

Success is a relatively poor teacher. Success confirms what you're already doing and gives you little incentive to change it. Success builds confidence, which is good, but it doesn't always build the kind of deep self-knowledge that makes you genuinely excellent over the long run. Success feels good. It's supposed to. But it doesn't ask the hard questions.

Failure asks the hard questions.

Failure asks: How do you respond when things don't go your way? Do you have the humility to honestly assess what went wrong, or does your pride get in the way? Can you receive criticism — from a coach, from film, from your own honest evaluation — without becoming defensive or despairing? Do you have the mental discipline to separate what happened from who you are? Do you have enough faith to trust that this hard moment is part of something larger?

Those questions, answered honestly and consistently over time, build something in an athlete that success alone cannot: genuine resilience. Not the performance of resilience — the chest-puffed, "I don't care about losses" performance that some athletes put on. Actual resilience, the kind that has been tested and held, the kind that has looked at real defeat and come back anyway.

Failure also builds humility. And humility, in an athlete, is quietly one of the most powerful competitive advantages available. The humble athlete knows what he doesn't know. He stays teachable. He receives coaching without the ego friction that makes development slow. He doesn't get too high after wins or too low after losses, which means his baseline performance stays more consistent. He builds real relationships with teammates because he isn't performing invincibility all the time — he's actually human, and humans trust other humans.

Failure builds compassion, too — something that sounds soft but matters for leadership. The athlete who has been through real difficulty, real disappointment, real setbacks — he knows what it feels like from the inside. When a teammate is struggling, he doesn't just offer a surface-level encouragement. He actually gets it. And that understanding is the foundation of real team culture.

None of this glorifies failure. Losing is not the goal. Mistakes are not the point. You should still compete with everything you have to avoid them. But when they happen — and they will — you can take something from them that compounds over time into a version of you that is genuinely stronger, more capable, and more mature than the version that only ever knew success.

## THE ATHLETE WHO HAS LEARNED HOW TO FAIL WELL IS DANGEROUS. BECAUSE NOTHING CAN FINALLY STOP HIM.

**Peter and the Next Play**

There is a figure in the New Testament who, if he were a modern athlete, would be one of the most relatable characters in the locker room. His name is Peter, and his story is a masterclass in failure, shame, grace, and recovery.

Peter was one of Jesus's closest friends and disciples. He was bold, passionate, emotionally intense — the kind of guy who jumps out of the boat and starts walking on water before he thinks through the implications, the kind of guy who cuts off a soldier's ear with a sword when the guards come to arrest

Jesus because he just can't stand there and do nothing. His heart was enormous and his commitment was fierce.

And then came the worst night of his life.

After Jesus was arrested, Peter followed at a distance into the courtyard of the high priest. Three times that night, different people identified Peter as one of Jesus's followers. Three times, Peter denied it. The third time, the rooster crowed — just as Jesus had predicted — and Peter remembered what Jesus had told him: before the rooster crows, you will deny me three times. Luke 22:62 records what happened next: And he went outside and wept bitterly.

If there was ever a moment that looked like the end of a story, that was it. The passionate, committed, bold disciple — the one who had declared that even if everyone else fell away, he never would — had publicly denied knowing Jesus. Three times. In the worst moment, when it cost something real to stand up, he hadn't.

But the story doesn't end there. Because grace never ends the story there.

After the resurrection, Jesus specifically sought Peter out. John 21 records the scene by the Sea of Galilee — a charcoal fire on the beach, fish cooking, and Jesus asking Peter the same question three times: Do you love me? The repetition wasn't cruelty. It was intentional restoration. For each denial, a declaration. For each failure, a re-commissioning. For each moment of shameful collapse, a specific and personal affirmation that the failure was not the final chapter.

Feed my sheep. Take care of my lambs. The man who had denied Jesus three times on the worst night in human history was given a purpose that extended far beyond that night. His failure was real. The shame was real. But the grace was bigger than the shame, and the restoration was specific, personal, and complete.

You are not Peter — your stakes are different, your story is your own. But the pattern is the same. You will have your worst nights. You will have moments where you let down the people who believed in you, where you didn't show up the way you know you should have, where the gap between who you want to be and who you were in that moment feels wide enough to swallow you.

Grace is bigger than the gap.

The next play is always available. Not because the last play didn't matter, but because the One who defines your worth has already decided that the last play doesn't get the final word.

## YOU DON'T HAVE TO STAY THERE

After the bad game. After the missed shot, the turnover, the blown assignment, the loss that hurt more than you expected, the slump that has gone on longer than you thought it would. After the replay that ran on a loop all Sunday night. After the Monday where you walked into school carrying something heavy that nobody else could see.

You don't have to stay there.

That is not the same as saying it doesn't matter. It did matter. It still matters. The pain is real. The disappointment is legitimate. You are allowed to feel it completely, without rushing past it to forced positivity. Honest grief over a genuine loss is not weakness. It's humanity.

But honest grief is different from indefinite residence. You can feel the loss, process it, learn what it has to teach you, and then choose to move. Not because you've manufactured enough willpower to force it. But because you have a foundation that the loss didn't touch. An identity that survived the mistake. A God who is already in your next game, your next season, your next opportunity to compete — who is not looking at you with the face of a disappointed evaluator, but with the face of someone who knew this was coming and is still completely committed to you.

The next play is always available to you. Not because of talent, or work ethic, or mental strength alone — but because the grace that covers your worst plays is unlimited. Because the One who knows every mistake you've ever made and every one you haven't made yet is still saying: come on. We're not done. Next play.

*"But one thing I do: Forgetting what is behind and straining toward what is ahead, I press on toward the goal to win the prize for which God has called me heavenward in Christ Jesus." — **Philippians 3:13–14***

Paul wrote that from prison. His past included having persecuted and helped kill the very people he later gave his life to serve. He had failures on his record that were far more serious than a bad game. And his instruction is not to minimize the past or pretend it didn't happen — it's to refuse to let it determine the direction of your forward movement.

Forget what is behind. Strain toward what is ahead. Press on.

That is the next-play mindset at its deepest level. Not a coaching cliché, but a theological statement. The past is not the frame that defines the future. The grace that covers what's behind you is also the energy that propels what's in front of you.

So get back on the field.

You've got a next play waiting.

## A PRAYER FOR THIS MOMENT

*God, I need help with this one. I'm carrying mistakes — some from today, some from last week, some that I've been dragging around longer than I want to admit. And I'm tired of how heavy they are.*

*Help me understand the difference between healthy reflection and the spiral. Help me learn from my failures without being defined by them. Help me extend to myself some of the grace that You extend to me — not to excuse the mistakes, but to free me from the weight of them.*

*Teach me the next-play mindset from the inside out, not just as a phrase but as a real way of competing. When the mistake happens and the spiral starts, remind me to acknowledge, release, redirect, and return to truth. Help me practice that until it's fast and automatic.*

*And on the days when the slump won't break and the results won't come — remind me that You are still working. That this isn't abandoned time. That something is being built in me that I might not be able to see yet.*

*I trust You with my failures. That might be the hardest kind of trust. But it's the kind that changes everything. Amen.*

# THINK ON THIS

1. Think of a specific mistake or bad game from the recent past that you are still carrying. What would it look like to fully process it and release it?

2. Where do you recognize your own spiral pattern? What does it usually look like — overthinking, anger, forcing plays, shutting down? What triggers it most often?

3. Is there a difference between how you respond to your own mistakes and how you respond to a teammate's mistakes? What does that tell you?

4. What has a hard loss or difficult season taught you that a win never could have? Name something specific.

# GAME-DAY CHALLENGE

This week, build your personal next-play reset.

Step 1: Choose a physical anchor — one small gesture (a breath, a tap on the chest, a shake of the hands) that will signal your brain to reset. Practice it when you're calm, so it s available when you're not.

Step 2: Write a one-sentence truth statement you can say to yourself after a mistake. Keep it short, grounded, and honest. Something like: "That play is over. I compete in the present." Or: "My identity is not in that play."

Step 3: The next time a mistake happens in practice or competition, walk through acknowledge — release — redirect — truth. Don't try to be perfect at it. Just notice what happens when you try.

Track over the next two weeks: are you recovering faster? Is the spiral shortening? Are you staying present longer after mistakes? Small improvements in this area compound into a significantly different competitor over a season.

# CHAPTER 4
# BUILT ON DISCIPLINE

DAILY HABITS *That Make You Stronger*

*"No discipline seems pleasant at the time, but painful. Later on, however, it produces a harvest of righteousness and peace for those who have been trained by it."* — *Hebrews 12:11*

# THE FEELING NOBODY TALKS ABOUT

Here is a scenario that almost every athlete has lived through at least once.

It is the week before the big game, or the night before a hard practice, or the morning of a conditioning session that you have been dreading since it was announced. And you wake up, and the feeling is just not there. The energy, the drive, the fire — the thing you felt in abundance two weeks ago when the season was fresh and everything felt possible — it is nowhere to be found. You are staring at the ceiling and the honest truth is that you would genuinely rather be doing almost anything else than what you are about to go do.

And here is the question that separates athletes more than almost any talent differential ever will: what do you do with that feeling?

Do you negotiate with it? Roll over and let the alarm go back to snooze? Tell yourself you'll make up for it tomorrow, that one missed rep or one half-effort practice won't matter in the larger scheme of things? Or do you get up anyway — not because you feel like it, but because you made a commitment to the process, and the process doesn't pause for your mood?

This is not a small question. It is, in a lot of ways, the question that determines what kind of athlete you become. And more than that — it is the question that starts shaping what kind of man you become.

Motivation is real and it's valuable. When motivation is present, training feels electric. The extra rep doesn't hurt as much. The film session doesn't drag. The early morning feels worth it because the excitement of the goal is buzzing in your chest like a live wire. That feeling is great. Enjoy it when it shows up.

But motivation is a visitor, not a resident. It comes and goes without announcing itself, shows up unpredictably, and has absolutely no obligation to be present when you need it most. If your effort level depends on whether motivation has decided to show up today, your consistency will be as unreliable as the weather — and your growth will follow suit.

Discipline is different. Discipline is not a feeling. It is a decision you make in advance and then honor, repeatedly, regardless of how you feel in the moment. Discipline is what gets you to practice when motivation hasn't checked in. It's what makes you watch the film when you'd rather watch anything else. It's what keeps your effort honest even when no coach is watching, even when nobody would know if you cut the corner, even when the path of least resistance is right there and very tempting.

Discipline is not glamorous. It doesn't usually feel inspiring while it's happening. But over time, it builds something that motivation alone never could: a deep, quiet confidence that comes from knowing you showed up when it was hard, that your preparation was honest, that when the pressure arrives, you have something real to stand on.

This chapter is about that. About how habits shape athletes and young men. About why the small daily choices matter more than any single inspirational moment. And about how discipline — the athletic kind and the spiritual kind — connects in ways that make both stronger.

# THE ATHLETE YOU'RE BECOMING RIGHT NOW

Every day you practice, you are making a deposit. You may not be able to see it. The improvement from Tuesday to Wednesday is probably invisible. Your vertical is not measurably higher after one good lift. Your shooting percentage does not noticeably improve after one focused session at the gym. Single deposits are small.

But compounding works in athletics the same way it works in finance. The deposits accumulate. The skills that feel slow to develop suddenly consolidate. The athlete who has been quietly putting in honest work for six months looks meaningfully different from the one who hasn't — not because of one dramatic training session, but because of two hundred small, unsexy, nobody's-watching sessions that compounded into genuine improvement.

Here is what is true right now, whether it feels true or not: the athlete you are becoming is being shaped by your daily habits more than by any other single factor. More than your natural talent. More than the quality of your coaching. More than whether you were born with the right build for your sport. Your habits — what you do consistently, when it would be easier not to — are writing the story of the athlete you are going to be.

That is both sobering and exciting. Sobering because it means there is no way around the daily work. No shortcut past the unglamorous repetitions. No life hack that replaces honest effort over time. Exciting because it means the trajectory is genuinely in your hands. You are not stuck with whatever you were born with. You are not at the mercy of circumstances you cannot control. Every day, in small and concrete ways, you get to decide what you are building.

**What are the habits that build?**

Showing up — consistently, on time, prepared to work — seems obvious, but it is not universal. The athlete who is reliably present, reliably prepared, reliably focused creates something over a career that the athlete who shows up randomly never does: a track record of reliability. Coaches notice. Teammates notice. And over time, you notice, too, in the way your confidence deepens when you know that you have been genuinely present for the process.

Listening actively — actually processing what coaches say instead of just being physically present while mentally elsewhere — is a habit that accelerates development at a rate that is genuinely hard to overstate. The athlete who listens gets the same coaching as the one who doesn't, but he actually integrates it. He improves faster. He makes fewer repeated mistakes. He earns trust more quickly. And he doesn't waste his own time pretending to absorb input he is not actually absorbing.

Practicing with intention — not just going through motions, but bringing cognitive engagement to every repetition — is the difference between hours spent and hours invested. You can accumulate a lot of time in a sport without accumulating a proportional amount of skill if the time is spent on autopilot. The athlete who asks himself what he is specifically working on and why, who tries to feel the difference between a well-executed rep and a sloppy one, who uses practice as an actual laboratory for improvement — that athlete gets more out of every hour than the one who is just waiting for practice to end.

Recovering well — sleep, nutrition, physical recovery, emotional reset after hard days — is the unsexy underside of athletic development that young athletes routinely underinvest in. The body and mind adapt during recovery, not during the training itself. An athlete who trains hard and recovers poorly is leaving significant performance on the table. And an athlete who is chronically sleep-deprived — which describes a startling percentage of teen athletes — is operating with measurably impaired cognition, reaction time, emotional regulation, and learning capacity. Getting enough sleep is not soft. It is science.

## YOU DON'T RISE TO THE LEVEL OF YOUR GOALS. YOU FALL TO THE LEVEL OF YOUR HABITS.

That idea is not original — coaches and performance researchers have been saying versions of it for decades. But it is consistently underestimated by young athletes who are focused on big goals without being equally focused on the daily habits that make those goals achievable. The goal is the destination. The habits are the road. You cannot reach the destination without traveling the road, no matter how clearly you can picture where you want to end up.

## WHERE REAL CONFIDENCE ACTUALLY COMES FROM

In Chapter 1 we talked about pressure and how to handle it. Here is a piece of that puzzle that deserves its own spotlight: one of the most practical, reliable, and underutilized tools for managing pressure is preparation.

Real confidence — not arrogance, not false bravado, but the genuine, settled, ground-level confidence that holds up under pressure — is not primarily a mindset choice. It is not primarily an affirmation practice. It is not primarily something you talk yourself into the morning of the game. It is largely a product of your preparation history. Of whether, in your honest self-assessment, you know that you did the work.

Think about the difference in how you feel walking into a test you studied thoroughly versus a test you barely glanced at the night before. The knowledge in your head is materially different, yes. But the feeling in your chest is different too. When you are well-prepared, there is a steadiness. Not certainty — you can still be nervous, still feel pressure, still worry about specific questions you might not have covered. But underneath the nervousness is something solid. You showed up for this. You put the time in. Whatever happens, you did your part.

Now contrast that with the experience of walking into a high-stakes situation that you know, in your honest heart, you were not fully prepared for. The anxiety is a different flavor. More desperate. More fragile. Because the question is not just "can I handle the pressure" — it is "can I perform with a preparation deficit I am trying to hide?" That version of pressure is harder, heavier, and less manageable.

Athletes often look for the mental key to playing calm under pressure as though confidence is primarily a psychological puzzle. And the mental side matters enormously — this whole book is built on that. But the mental and the practical are not separate systems. They feed each other. Genuine preparation produces genuine confidence. And genuine confidence makes the mental work of managing pressure significantly more effective.

This does not mean that anxiety disappears when you're well-prepared. Elite athletes with decades of experience and thorough preparation still get nervous. But the anxiety sits on top of a prepared foundation instead of a hollow one. And that distinction makes an enormous practical difference.

The inverse is also true and worth being honest about. Poor preparation is one of the most direct creators of performance anxiety. When you know you cut corners — skipped the film session, coasted through practice on the days when the coach seemed distracted, let your conditioning slide, avoided the parts of your game that are weak instead of attacking them — the anxiety that arrives on game day is not irrational. It is an accurate reading of your preparation deficit. And no amount of pregame hype or motivational music is going to fully paper over the gap between where your preparation actually is and where you wish it was.

Discipline in preparation is, quite literally, an investment in your own mental health on game day. Every honest practice session is a deposit into the account of confidence. Every film session, every extra rep, every unglamorous physical maintenance habit — they all accumulate into the settled sense that you are ready. And being ready is one of the greatest gifts you can give yourself before the pressure arrives.

*"The plans of the diligent lead to profit as surely as haste leads to poverty."* — **Proverbs 21:5**

The diligent. Not the most talented. Not the most athletically gifted. Not the biggest or fastest or most naturally skilled. The diligent — those who plan and prepare and execute with consistency — are the ones who build something that lasts. The verse is written in the context of business, but the principle applies to every area of human endeavor that requires sustained effort over time. And athletic development is exactly that.

# THE QUIET THIEF: EXCUSES, SHORTCUTS, AND DOING THE MINIMUM

Let's have the honest conversation, because a book that only affirms you without occasionally challenging you isn't actually serving you.

Every athlete has a version of this: the practice where the effort was somewhere between adequate and lazy, but you told yourself a story afterward that made it feel acceptable. The film session you sat through while mostly thinking about something else. The extra work you said you would do after practice and then found seventeen reasons not to do. The early morning lift you slept through and justified with "I needed the rest" even though you went to bed at midnight for no particular reason.

These moments are normal. They happen to every athlete, including good ones, including disciplined ones. The question is not whether you ever have them — you will. The question is whether you are honest with yourself about them, and whether they are the exception or the pattern.

Here is what excuses actually cost you, and it's worth understanding clearly: every time you accept a convenient excuse for a substandard effort, you are making a small deposit into a different kind of account. Not the confidence account. The doubt account. Because somewhere underneath the excuse, your honest self knows. The brain is remarkably good at keeping an accurate record of whether you actually did the work, regardless of what story you tell yourself on the surface. And that accurate internal record — the one that doesn't care about your justifications — is what speaks to you on game day when the pressure is highest.

The athlete who has a habit of doing the minimum is not just less physically prepared than the one who consistently goes beyond it. He is less psychologically prepared. He does not have the foundation of honest effort to stand on when the pressure asks hard questions. And when the pressure asks hard questions — as it always does — he has to answer with whatever he actually built. Not what he meant to build. Not what he would have built if circumstances had been more convenient. What he actually, honestly built.

Shortcuts are a similar problem. In the short term, a shortcut looks efficient. You get the same output with less input. But the shortcuts that matter most in athletic development are not the ones that save you five minutes today. They are the ones that save you from the discomfort of the thing you most need to work on. The weak part of your game you avoid practicing because it's frustrating. The conditioning you skip because it hurts and the coach wasn't watching. The aspect of your technique that needs rebuilding from the ground up but that you patch with a compensating movement because the rebuild feels too hard and too slow.

Those shortcuts cost you exactly the growth you most need. They keep you stuck at the ceiling of your current ability while the athletes who attack their weaknesses are pushing through it.

And then there is blame — the cousin of excuses. Blame is what happens when honest accountability feels too uncomfortable. The bad game was because the coach put you in a bad position. The dropped ball was because the pass was slightly off. The conditioning you skipped was because your schedule is busier than anyone else's. The missed assignment in the film was because the scheme is complicated. All of these things can contain partial truths — sometimes the coach does make poor decisions, sometimes the schedule is genuinely full, sometimes schemes are genuinely complicated. But blame in its habitual form is not a search for partial truth. It's a protection strategy. It keeps your own role in your results at arm's length, which means it also keeps your agency at arm's length. Because you can only improve the things you honestly own.

## YOU OWN YOUR EFFORT.

*Which means you own your results. Which means you have more power over your development than any excuse will ever let you believe.*

The most liberating version of accountability is not self-punishment. It's honest ownership. I could have worked harder there. I avoided that weakness instead of addressing it. I was distracted in that session and I know it. Those honest admissions are not attacks on your worth — your worth is settled, as Chapter 2 established. They are simply accurate readings of effort that give you something real to work with going forward.

## SELF-CONTROL IS NOT WHAT YOU THINK IT IS

If you ask most teen athletes what self-control means, they will describe something that sounds like restriction. Not eating the food you want. Not staying up as late as you want. Not saying the thing you want to say when you're frustrated. A long list of deprivations, enforced by discipline, in the service of goals that sometimes feel abstract.

That frame makes self-control feel like a cage. And a cage is not motivating.

Here is a different frame, and it is both more accurate and significantly more motivating: self-control is the ability to choose the version of yourself you most want to be, even when a less-disciplined version is more immediately comfortable.

That's not a cage. That's power.

Think about what self-control actually produces in an athlete. It produces the ability to choose the early morning workout over the extra hour of sleep, not because sleep doesn't matter, but because this specific morning, this specific commitment matters more. It produces the ability to respond to a bad call with composure instead of a reaction that costs your team a penalty or a technical foul. It produces the ability to finish strong at the end of a conditioning session when your body is telling you to ease up, because you've decided that you are someone who finishes strong. It produces the ability to take constructive criticism from a coach and integrate it instead of getting defensive, because you've decided that growth matters more than protecting your ego.

None of those things feel like freedom in the moment of choosing them. But they produce freedom — the freedom of a disciplined athlete who has more options, more confidence, more trust from his coaches and teammates, and a wider ceiling on his own development than the undisciplined version of himself ever would have.

Self-control in competition specifically is worth its own attention. The emotionally reactive athlete — the one who fires back at trash talk, who argues calls instead of returning to focus, who lets frustration with a teammate's mistake affect his own performance, who melts down after being benched — is burning energy that should be going toward competing. Emotion management is not about suppressing feeling. It's about choosing which feelings get to direct your behavior and which ones you let pass through without acting on.

The athlete who can be genuinely angry about a bad call and still make the next play with full effort and composure — that is not someone who doesn't care. That is someone with a level of emotional intelligence and self-regulation that is genuinely rare and genuinely valuable. It doesn't happen automatically. It is trained, like a physical skill, through repeated practice over time.

*"Like a city whose walls are broken through is a person who lacks self-control."* — **Proverbs 25:28**

A city without walls is vulnerable. Any invader can walk straight in, and nothing inside is protected. That is the image Proverbs uses for a person without self-control — exposed, undefended, at the mercy of whatever comes at him from outside. Emotions, impulses, distractions, provocations — they all get in, and they all have an equal claim on how he responds.

The athlete with genuine self-control has walls. Not walls that keep him emotionally numb or unavailable — but walls that mean he chooses what gets inside, what gets to direct his behavior, what he allows to have authority over his focus and his effort. That protection is not a limitation. It is a form of genuine strength.

Galatians 5:22–23 lists self-control as one of the fruits of the Spirit — the natural outgrowth of a life genuinely connected to God. That framing is significant. Self-control is not generated purely from personal willpower. For the Christian athlete, it is cultivated through the ongoing practice of a faith that shapes character from the inside out. Which is a natural bridge to the next part of this conversation.

# *TRAINING THE BODY AND TRAINING THE SOUL*

Paul, who wrote a significant portion of the New Testament, knew athletes. The Greek and Roman cultures in which he lived were soaked in athletic competition — the Olympic Games were ancient even in Paul's time, and athletic metaphors were a natural part of the cultural vocabulary. He used them freely and, it seems, with genuine appreciation for what athletic training reveals about disciplined human effort.

In 1 Corinthians 9:24–27, he writes: Do you not know that in a race all the runners run, but only one gets the prize? Run in such a way as to get the prize. Everyone who competes in the games goes into strict training. They do it to get a crown that will not last, but we do it to get a crown that will last forever.

The observation at the center of that passage is worth sitting with: everyone who competes in the games goes into strict training. Paul is not describing the elite athletes or the exceptionally dedicated — he is describing everyone who shows up to compete at all. Strict training is the baseline. It is what competition requires. And his point is not to criticize athletic discipline but to elevate it: if athletes put this much effort into something temporary, how much more serious should the pursuit of something eternal be?

But the parallel runs both directions. Paul is also, implicitly, drawing a connection between the discipline of athletic training and the discipline of spiritual formation. Both require consistent effort. Both involve repetition that doesn't always feel inspiring. Both produce results that are invisible in the short term and unmistakable in the long term. Both require showing up when motivation is absent and doing the work because commitment and character demand it.

Athletic discipline and spiritual discipline are not rivals for your time and attention. They are complementary. They reinforce each other. The habits of self-regulation and consistency that you build through athletic training make you more capable of spiritual discipline. And the character, identity, and peace that spiritual discipline produces make you a more grounded, more resilient, more purposeful athlete.

What does spiritual discipline actually look like for a teen athlete in a busy, demanding season? Not necessarily long church services and extended quiet times every morning, though those things have their place. For a young athlete in the middle of a demanding schedule, spiritual discipline might look like:

A consistent morning check-in with God — something as simple as a one-minute acknowledgment of the day, a brief expression of gratitude for the ability to compete, a short honest prayer about what you're carrying into the day. Two minutes. Done before you pick up your phone. That practice, done consistently over a season, is not nothing. It is a daily act of orientation — a reminder of who you are and whose you are before the day's demands start defining the terms.

A consistent practice of taking Scripture with you into sports contexts. Not carrying a Bible onto the court — just carrying a verse into the week. One verse that speaks to what you're actually dealing with. Pressure: Philippians 4:7. Identity after failure: Isaiah 43:1. The call to disciplined effort: Colossians 3:23. Keeping one truth in your mental back pocket during a hard week is not complicated. And it changes the texture of the week in ways that are hard to fully articulate until you've tried it.

Honest conversation with God after hard days. Not polished prayer — honest prayer. God, I was frustrated today and I didn't handle it well. I'm tired and I don't feel like I have much left. I need You to do something in this that I can't do on my own. That kind of honesty is more valuable than theologically correct language delivered from behind emotional armor. God does not need your performance. He wants your presence.

Gratitude as a daily habit. Gratitude is one of the most consistently documented psychological interventions available — it actually shifts mood and cognitive perspective in measurable ways. But beyond the psychology, it is a theological practice: the regular acknowledgment that your ability is a gift, that the opportunity to compete is not guaranteed, that there are people who would give a lot to be in the position you're in. Gratitude does not erase frustration or difficulty. But it keeps the frustration in its proper place relative to everything else that is also true.

# THE REAL TEST: WHO YOU ARE WHEN NOBODY IS WATCHING

There is a version of discipline that most athletes can access when the stakes are visible. When the coach is watching, the effort goes up. When the scout is in the stands, technique tightens. When the game matters, focus sharpens. That version of discipline is fine — it's responsive to external motivation, and external motivation is not worthless.

But the version of discipline that actually shapes character — the version that builds something permanent — is the kind that shows up when nobody is watching. When the coach stepped away and the reps could easily be cut short. When the film session could be half-attended because the coaching staff isn't checking. When the extra work after practice is entirely optional and nobody will know whether you did it or not.

Who are you in those moments? That question is not rhetorical. It is the most honest measure of the kind of athlete and young man you are actually becoming — more honest than your stats, more honest than your coaches' assessment of you, more honest than what your teammates see.

The hidden moments matter for a reason that goes beyond athletic development, though they shape that too. They matter because integrity — the alignment between what you profess to be and what you actually do when the audience disappears — is one of the foundational character qualities of a man who can be trusted. And being trusted — by coaches, by teammates, by the people in your life who matter — is not just a nice social outcome. It is the prerequisite for leadership, for real relationships, for the kind of influence that actually changes things.

An athlete who works hard in front of coaches and coasts when they're gone is not building integrity. He is building a performance. And performances are fragile, because they require an audience. The moment the audience disappears, the performance stops. But integrity doesn't require an audience. Integrity does the same thing regardless of who is watching, because integrity is not about being seen — it is about being who you said you are.

Luke 16:10 says: Whoever can be trusted with very little can also be trusted with much, and whoever is dishonest with very little will also be dishonest with much. The principle of faithfulness in small things applies directly to the hidden habits of an athlete. The Tuesday afternoon rep when the coach is gone. The nutrition choice when nobody is monitoring it. The mental preparation work that happens in your own head before a game. The attitude in the weight room on a Saturday when only the most committed guys are there.

Those small, unseen faithfulnesses accumulate. They shape the athlete you are in the visible moments. They build the kind of trust that coaches give responsibility to. And they form the kind of character that has something to stand on when the pressure of the big moments arrives.

## THE ATHLETE YOU ARE IN PRIVATE IS THE ATHLETE YOU WILL BE UNDER PRESSURE.

*The private habits write the public performance.*

That connection is real and it runs deep. If your honest private practice is different from what people see when coaches are watching, the gap between those two versions will eventually make itself known — in the moments when pressure calls on what is actually there, not what was performed for an audience.

The goal is no gap. The goal is an athlete whose visible effort and invisible effort are the same, because the effort is not for the coach's approval or the parent's praise. The effort is for something larger: the pursuit of genuine excellence, the honoring of a gift you've been given, and the integrity of a young man who has decided that who he is matters more than who he appears to be.

## THE MOST UNDERRATED QUALITY ON ANY TEAM

Ask a coach what they value most in a player and the answers will vary: athleticism, work ethic, coachability, leadership, competitiveness. Different coaches, different sports, different answers. But dig a little deeper and there is one quality that almost every coach will name as foundational, the quality that makes everything else possible:

Dependability.

The athlete who shows up. Who does his job, consistently, even when the adrenaline of early-season enthusiasm has worn off and practice feels like a grind. Who brings the same preparation and the same attitude on a random Wednesday in February as he does for the opener in September. Whose teammates can count on him to execute his assignment, to be where he is supposed to be, to give what he committed to give.

That athlete is invaluable. Not necessarily because he is the most talented. Not because his highlight reel is the most impressive. But because he is real. What you see is what you get, and what you get is reliable.

Dependability is the direct product of discipline. You cannot be dependable on talent alone — talent fluctuates, gets injured, has bad nights. You cannot be dependable on enthusiasm alone — enthusiasm runs hot and cool and doesn't show up on demand. Dependability requires the kind of consistent disciplined effort that shows up day after day because the person has made a decision about who he is going to be, regardless of how he feels.

For young athletes, dependability is one of the fastest paths to increased responsibility and trust. Coaches give playing time, roles, and leadership positions to athletes they can count on, not always to the most gifted athletes in the room. The naturally talented but inconsistent player creates anxiety for a coaching staff — you never know which version you're getting. The less-gifted but deeply reliable player creates confidence — you know exactly what you're getting, and you can build around it.

Dependability also makes you a better teammate in ways that go beyond individual performance. Teams with reliable people experience less relational friction. When everyone trusts each other to show up and do their job, the emotional energy that might otherwise go into frustration and disappointment stays available for competing. Trust between teammates is not built in locker room speeches. It is built over hundreds of practices where people consistently did what they said they would do.

Being dependable is also a form of service. Your teammates are counting on you to be present and prepared. Your coaches are counting on your execution within the scheme. When you honor those dependencies, you are not just serving your own development — you are contributing to something larger than yourself. And the habit of serving something larger than yourself, practiced in the specific context of your sport, is one of the most valuable habits you can build as a young man.

## YOU ARE WHAT YOU REPEATEDLY DO

There is a famous line — variously attributed but most often credited to Aristotle — that goes something like this: We are what we repeatedly do. Excellence, then, is not an act but a habit.

This connects directly to everything in this book about identity, because it means that identity is not only something that is given to you — though it is that, in the most fundamental sense, as Chapters 2 and 3 established. Identity is also something that is being shaped by your repeated actions. Who you are becoming is, in significant part, a function of what you do every day.

The athlete who consistently works hard in hidden moments is not just building better physical skills. He is becoming someone who works hard in hidden moments — and that character quality does not stay confined to his sport. It transfers. It shows up in how he approaches school, how he treats people who can do nothing for him, how he responds to difficulty in areas that have nothing to do with competition. Character built in the athletic context is character built for life.

The reverse is also true. The habits of excuse-making, shortcuts, and doing the minimum that some athletes develop in their sports career do not stay in the locker room when the season ends. They migrate. They become the operating mode for whatever comes next: college, work, relationships, responsibility. Every season of athletic competition is simultaneously a season of character formation — and the character being formed will outlast the sport by decades.

This is why the stakes of discipline are higher than they might appear from the outside. On the surface, it looks like the question is just about whether you're going to be a good athlete. Underneath, it is also about whether you are going to be a person who can be trusted, who shows up when it costs something, who finishes what they start, who does what they said they would do. Those are not athletic qualities. Those are human qualities that matter everywhere, forever.

*"Whatever you do, work at it with all your heart, as working for the Lord, not for human masters." — **Colossians 3:23***

With all your heart. Not with most of it. Not with enough of it to get by. All of it. And the motivation that makes all-heart effort sustainable is not external performance pressure but something deeper: working as for the Lord. Competing, training, and preparing with the awareness that your effort is an act of honoring the One who gave you this body, this ability, this opportunity.

That framing changes the entire quality of your effort. When you are working for the approval of coaches, you work hard when they are watching and ease up when they are not. When you are working for statistics, you work hardest in the situations that generate visible numbers and coast through the ones that don't. When you are working as for the Lord — when the underlying purpose of your effort is to honor God with everything you have — the effort doesn't require an audience. It doesn't depend on whether the performance shows up in the box score. It is consistent because the purpose behind it is consistent.

That is the deepest foundation of discipline: not personal ambition, not fear of falling behind, but the understanding that your daily effort is a form of stewardship. You have been given something — ability, opportunity, time, physical capacity. The disciplined use of that gift is an act of gratitude and worship. The careless waste of it is something less.

# HABITS THAT ACTUALLY MOVE THE NEEDLE

Let's bring this down to the ground level. Here are specific, practical habits that compound over a season into genuine athletic and character development. These are not revolutionary. They are simple. The simplicity is the point — because simple habits, consistently practiced, beat complicated systems that never get implemented.

Before practice or a game: take two minutes to set an intention. What specifically are you working on today? What is the one thing you most want to improve or execute? Going into a session with a specific focus point creates a different quality of engagement than just showing up and going through the motions. It also gives you something concrete to evaluate afterward — did I do what I came here to do?

After practice: spend three minutes in honest review. Not an extended self-critique session — just a brief, honest look at what happened. What went well? What needs work? What will you do differently tomorrow? This habit, done consistently, accelerates development at a rate that pure repetition without reflection never matches. You are turning experience into learning instead of just accumulating time.

Before sleep: write down or say out loud three specific things you are grateful for about today. They don't have to be big. The ability to train. A moment of good chemistry with a teammate. A rep that felt right. The fact that your body is functional and capable. This practice is not a happiness hack — it is the regular exercise of a perspective that keeps the hard days from defining your whole experience of the season.

Weekly: take five minutes with a verse that speaks to where you actually are. Not a random verse-of-the-day — a verse that addresses what you are actually carrying. Under pressure? Philippians 4:6–7. In a slump? Isaiah 40:29–31. Struggling with comparison? Galatians 6:4. Processing a bad loss? Romans 8:28. Bring the real stuff to Scripture and let it speak to the real stuff.

Daily: protect your sleep. This one is the most consistently ignored habit by teen athletes and the one with the largest measurable return on investment. Between seven and nine hours for teens is not laziness. It is the recovery window during which your body actually adapts to training, your brain consolidates skills and learning, your emotional regulation systems reset, and your focus for the next day is restored. Athletes who consistently undersleep consistently underperform relative to their potential, regardless of how hard they train when they're awake.

In moments of frustration: pause before responding. One breath. That's all. Between the emotion and the reaction, create one breath of space. In that space, ask: what response would I be proud of in ten minutes? What response reflects who I actually want to be? That one breath, consistently practiced, prevents a significant percentage of the unnecessary reactions that cost athletes penalties, ejections, teammate friction, and coaching trust. It sounds almost too small to matter. In game situations, it matters enormously.

None of these habits require extra equipment, extra money, or extra hours in your day. They require attention and intention — the decision to bring a little more awareness and a little more consistency to things you are already doing. That is the unsexy truth of habit formation: the gains come not from doing spectacular new things but from doing small existing things with more honesty and more care.

## DANIEL AND THE DISCIPLINE OF QUIET FAITHFULNESS

If you want a biblical model for the kind of disciplined, consistent, private-integrity character this chapter is describing, look at Daniel.

Daniel was a young man — probably a teenager — when he was taken from Jerusalem to Babylon as part of a foreign conquest. He was brought into the Babylonian court for training, given a new name, offered the food and wine of the king's table, and immersed in the language and literature of an empire that did not share his values or his God. The pressure to assimilate was enormous. The incentive to comply was real. The cost of standing out was significant.

Daniel resolved not to defile himself with the royal food and wine. That resolution, recorded in Daniel 1:8, sounds simple. It was not. It was a decision made quietly, without audience or applause, in the face of significant institutional pressure, at an age when most young people lack the formed character to make that kind of stand at all. He didn't make a scene. He didn't preach at anyone. He just quietly, consistently, maintained his convictions.

And then he asked for ten days to prove that his way worked.

At the end of ten days he looked healthier and better nourished than any of the young men who ate the royal food. At the end of the full training period, Daniel and his three friends were found to be ten times better than all the magicians and enchanters in the whole kingdom. The private discipline, the quiet faithfulness, the daily habits maintained without fanfare — they produced results that were visible and undeniable.

You are probably not being tested with royal food in Babylon. But the principle of Daniel's story applies to your situation with remarkable precision. You are a young man in a culture that has its own forms of pressure and conformity. You have convictions — about effort, about integrity, about who you want to be and why — that are regularly tested by the easier path. The question of whether you maintain those convictions in the daily, private, unglamorous moments is the same question Daniel faced.

And the trajectory of Daniel's life suggests that the answer to that question, compounded over time, builds something extraordinary. Not just athletic excellence — Daniel's story goes far beyond athletic performance. But genuine excellence of character, the kind that holds up under pressure, that earns the trust of people who are watching carefully, that produces results that speak for themselves.

Quiet faithfulness. Consistent private discipline. Resolved convictions maintained without needing an audience. That is not boring. That is how great men are built.

# THE DAILY DECISION THAT CHANGES EVERYTHING

You will not become the athlete or the man you want to be in a single dramatic moment. You will not find the inspiration that permanently solves the motivation problem. You will not stumble across the life hack that makes discipline effortless. Those things are not real, and waiting for them is how years of potential get quietly wasted.

What you will have, every single day, is a choice. A small, unglamorous, often-uncomfortable choice to show up for the process. To do the work honestly. To be who you said you are even when the audience is absent. To bring your best to the session that nobody is evaluating. To take the long road of genuine preparation instead of the shortcut road of convenient justifications.

That choice, made today and again tomorrow and again next week, compounds. The athlete who makes it consistently for a full season looks different from the one who doesn't. The athlete who makes it consistently for a full year looks significantly different. The young man who makes it consistently through his formative years — in his sport, in his faith, in his character — becomes someone who has something real to stand on, not just something to perform.

Discipline is not punishment. It is not a restriction imposed on you from outside. At its best, it is the expression of a decision you have made about who you want to become — and the daily commitment to close the gap between where you are and where you're going. Every honest rep is a vote for the athlete you're becoming. Every private faithfulness is a vote for the man you're becoming. Every small act of self-control is a vote for the leader you have the potential to be.

You are not building toward a single moment. You are building an athlete, and more importantly, a person. The construction happens every day, in the hidden moments, in the consistent choices, in the habits that nobody applauds and that eventually produce something that everyone can see.

Start with today. Start with this session. Start with the next rep.

That is enough. And it is everything.

# A PRAYER FOR THIS MOMENT

*God, I want to be honest: I don't always feel disciplined. I feel motivated sometimes, and those days are great. But I also have days when I really don't feel like it, and those are the days I need this most.*

*Help me build the kind of discipline that doesn't depend on feelings. Help me show up for the process even when the excitement is gone. Help me bring honest effort to the hidden moments — the ones where nobody is watching and it would be easy to coast.*

*Help me understand that every rep I take seriously, every private habit I honor, every moment of self-control I choose — they are adding up to something real. Even when I can't see it.*

*And help me connect my athletic discipline to my spiritual discipline. Help me be as consistent in my faith habits as I want to be in my training habits. Let the two reinforce each other.*

*Teach me to work as for You, not for applause or statistics or anyone else's approval. That kind of purpose is the only kind that keeps going when everything else runs out.*

*I want to become someone who can be trusted. I want to be dependable. I want my private effort to match my public appearance. Help me close that gap, one day at a time. Amen.*

# THINK ON THIS

1. Be honest: is your effort level different when the coach is watching vs. when they're not? What does the gap (if there is one) tell you about what's actually driving your effort?

2. What is the one part of your game or your preparation that you most consistently avoid because it's uncomfortable? What would it look like to attack it this week?

3. Which specific spiritual habits — prayer, Scripture, gratitude — are most consistently absent from your daily routine? What is one small step toward making one of them regular?

4. Think of the most dependable athlete you know personally. What habits do you observe in them? What can you learn from watching how they operate day to day?

# GAME-DAY CHALLENGE

This week, pick ONE habit from each of these three categories and commit to it for seven days straight:

Athletic: Choose one specific thing you will do at every practice this week that is beyond the minimum — one extra rep, one additional film review, one aspect of your game you will consciously work on. Keep it specific and trackable.

Mental: Before each practice or game this week, take 60 seconds to set a specific intention. Write it down if you can. After the session, spend 60 seconds reviewing whether you followed through. That's it — two minutes total, per session.

Spiritual: Every morning this week, before you pick up your phone, say one honest sentence to God. It doesn't have to be eloquent. Just real. Gratitude, request, acknowledgment — whatever is true for you that morning.

At the end of the seven days, notice: did anything shift? Did your confidence going into practice feel different when you arrived with an intention? Did the morning check-in change the tone of even one difficult day?

Small experiments tell the truth. Run this one and see what the data says.

# CHAPTER 5
# LOCKER ROOM STRENGTH

## LEADERSHIP, *Respect, and Team Character*

*"Do nothing out of selfish ambition or vain conceit. Rather, in humility value others above yourselves, not looking to your own interests but each of you to the interests of the others." — Philippians 2:3–4*

# WHAT LEADERSHIP ACTUALLY LOOKS LIKE

Think about the leaders you have respected most in sports. Not the ones who talked the most or wore the captain's patch or had the most impressive stats. Think about the ones who actually changed something — the ones whose presence made the team feel different, made practice feel more serious, made a losing huddle feel like it still had a pulse.

Chances are, those people did not lead primarily through speeches. They led through something quieter and more consistent. The way they showed up every day regardless of how they felt. The way they responded after a mistake — briefly, cleanly, without drama. The way they stayed locked in when the game was going badly and everyone else wanted to mentally check out. The way they treated the freshman who was nervous in his first week and the senior who had been around forever. The way they carried themselves in the locker room, on the bus, in the film session when nothing important seemed to be happening.

That's leadership. Not a title. Not a volume level. Not a highlight-reel stat line. A consistent pattern of behavior, repeated over time, that builds something in the culture around them — trust, steadiness, belief, and the willingness to follow.

A lot of young athletes have a distorted picture of leadership because the leadership they see most publicly is often loud and dramatic. The sideline explosion. The emotional speech in the huddle. The captain who demands the ball in the big moment and delivers. Those moments are real and sometimes genuinely powerful. But they're not the foundation of leadership. They're the occasional visible expression of something that was built quietly, in practice, over months.

The foundation of real leadership is character. And character, as Chapter 4 established, is built in daily habits — in the private moments, the unglamorous ones, the moments that nobody is scoring or evaluating. The same principle applies when the question is not just about your individual development but about how you show up for the people around you.

You do not have to be the best player on your team to lead. You do not have to be the loudest voice in the room. You do not even have to have a formal leadership role. Leadership is available to every athlete on every team at every level, because leadership is fundamentally about the quality of your character in relationship with others — and that is something anyone can develop, regardless of their position on the depth chart.

This chapter is about that kind of leadership. The kind that grows in locker rooms and practice facilities, in bus rides and postgame huddles. The kind that shows up in how you treat people, how you respond to adversity, how you carry your body language, how you speak to teammates, and what you choose to be when nobody is watching but everybody is feeling.

## YOUR ATTITUDE IS NEVER PRIVATE

Here is something most athletes don't fully realize until someone points it out directly: your attitude is always communicating, whether you intend it to or not.

You can say nothing. You can keep your thoughts entirely to yourself. You can stay physically present in the huddle, on the bench, in the film session, in the locker room after a bad loss. And your attitude is still broadcasting, loudly and clearly, to every teammate and coach in the vicinity.

It broadcasts through your body language. The shoulders that slump when the coach makes a play call you disagree with. The eyes that roll just barely — just enough — when a teammate makes a mistake. The jaw that tightens when you come off the field and the energy you carry back to the bench, the energy that says I am frustrated and I am not interested in pretending otherwise. The arms crossed in the huddle. The absence of eye contact with the coach who just benched you for a series.

It broadcasts through your effort fluctuations. The way your energy visibly drops when things aren't going your way. The rep in practice that you take at 70 percent because you are not feeling it today. The way you stop communicating with teammates when you're in your head about your own performance.

It broadcasts through your words — or the specific absence of them. The encouragement you don't give when a teammate is struggling. The silence after someone makes a mistake when a simple word of support would cost you nothing. The half-hearted response in the huddle when a coach is trying to rally the group.

Teams are far more emotionally interconnected than most athletes consciously realize. Emotion is genuinely contagious in group environments. One player's body language can shift the energy of an entire huddle in a matter of seconds. One person's visible frustration can give permission for the rest of the team to disengage. And conversely, one player's composure in a hard moment — the calmness, the steady eyes, the refusal to panic — can be the thing that holds a team together when everything is going sideways.

That means your attitude on a bad day is not a private matter. It is a contribution — positive or negative — to the emotional environment of your team. And every contribution compounds over time into the culture that everyone on the team lives inside.

## YOU ARE ALWAYS EITHER ADDING TO THE CULTURE OR SUBTRACTING FROM IT. THERE IS NO NEUTRAL.

That is a significant responsibility. And for the athlete who takes it seriously, it is also a significant opportunity. Because if attitude is contagious, then a young man with a consistently strong, grounded, steady attitude has more influence on the people around him than he probably realizes. Not because he is lecturing anyone. Not because he is making speeches. Just because he shows up the same way every day and the people around him feel it.

# YOUR BODY IS TALKING. IS IT SAYING THE RIGHT THINGS?

Body language is worth its own dedicated section because it is one of the most impactful and least discussed tools available to a competing athlete — both in terms of how it affects others and how it affects you.

We already covered in Chapter 4 how adopting intentionally strong posture after a mistake can actually begin to interrupt the psychological spiral. The same principle applies in the team context. How you carry your body in competition is not just a performance output — it is a form of communication that teammates read constantly and respond to.

The head-down, shoulders-collapsed body language after a mistake tells your teammates: I'm in trouble. I'm not okay. This might be affecting my next play. That communication, delivered nonverbally, does something to the team's confidence in you. Not because they're judging your character — they're your teammates, they're not evaluating you harshly. But because they're human, and they read physical signals instinctively. Collapsed body language reads as collapse, period. And a team that sees too much of it starts to feel the weight collectively.

The reverse is equally powerful. The player who makes a mistake and comes off the field with his head up, his eyes forward, his body language communicating something like: That happened. I'm over it. I'm ready for the next one — that player sends a completely different signal. He's not pretending the mistake didn't happen. He's not faking happiness about it. He's demonstrating, physically, that he is not going to let the last play contaminate the next one. And that demonstration steadies people. It gives the team permission to believe the same thing.

Think about what it feels like to be on the bench after a rough stretch when the guy who just came off looks devastated. Now think about what it feels like when the guy who just came off looks like he's already moved on and ready to go again. Same score. Same situation. Completely different team energy. The body language did that.

Strong body language in competition includes: keeping your head up after mistakes, maintaining eye contact with coaches when being corrected, staying physically animated and engaged even when you're on the bench, refusing to hang your head or drag your feet when things aren't going your way. These are all choices, not feelings. You don't have to feel confident to carry confident body language. The behavior comes first, and the feeling often follows — and in the meantime, the behavior is communicating something valuable to the people around you.

Slamming equipment is worth a specific mention, because it's a pattern that is more common and more costly than most young athletes realize. When you slam a helmet, throw a water bottle, smash a piece of equipment after a mistake or a bad call — you might feel like you're just releasing frustration, and the emotional release might feel momentarily satisfying. But what you are actually doing is broadcasting to everyone around you that your emotional regulation is not functioning in this moment. You are telling your teammates that the situation got to you. You are telling your coaches that your composure is fragile. And you are making the people around you feel less safe — less certain that you are going to be a stable presence for the rest of the competition. The equipment doesn't care. The team does.

## THE STRONGEST GUYS IN THE ROOM LIFT OTHERS

There is a cultural message in competitive sports that encouragement is soft. That the tough athletes are the ones who are all business, don't hand out compliments, and let performance speak for itself. That being emotionally supportive of teammates is somehow in tension with being a serious, hard-nosed competitor.

That message is wrong, and it is worth pushing back on directly.

Some of the mentally toughest, most respected athletes at every level are also the ones who are most consistent in their encouragement of teammates. Not because they're softies. Because they understand something important about how teams function and what it takes to get the most out of the people around them.

When a teammate is struggling — in a slump, having a bad practice, getting worked by an opponent, battling a confidence issue — the most valuable thing someone in that locker room can do is not pretend it isn't happening. It is to offer the specific, genuine, well-timed word or gesture that communicates: I see you. I believe in you. We're good. Those moments don't require much. A hand on the shoulder. A brief, direct statement of confidence. The decision to say something real instead of nothing at all.

Teams that encourage each other well compete differently than teams that don't. The emotional cost of mistakes is lower when you know your teammates are going to help you reset instead of go quiet or turn critical. The risk of trying something bold in a game is more manageable when you trust that if it doesn't work, your team is behind you rather than ready to assign blame. The physical and psychological demands of a hard season are more sustainable when you feel genuinely connected to the people going through it with you.

Encouragement also has a secondary effect that is easy to underestimate: it is one of the primary ways that insecurity gets addressed in a team environment. Insecurity — the quiet fear that you're not good enough, that your spot is not secure, that you don't quite belong — is extremely common in competitive sport and is one of the primary sources of the selfishness, jealousy, and comparison that pull teams apart. Consistent, genuine encouragement from trusted teammates does not eliminate insecurity, but it gives it less room to operate. When you feel genuinely supported, the worst version of insecurity — the defensive, jealous, everyone-is-a-competitor kind — has less power.

*"Therefore encourage one another and build each other up, just as in fact you are doing." — 1 Thessalonians 5:11*

Build each other up. That's a construction metaphor — active, ongoing, intentional work. Not passive niceness. Not waiting until someone has a breakdown to say something supportive. Regular, consistent, daily building. The kind that, compounded over a season, produces a team that is genuinely more than the sum of its individual parts.

Be the guy who does that. Not because you need the social credit. Because you understand that building your teammates up is part of how you win — and, more importantly, part of what makes the experience worth having.

# THE THING THAT QUIETLY TEARS TEAMS APART

Let's talk about selfishness — not the cartoonish, obvious kind where a player blatantly ignores open teammates to take bad shots, though that version exists too. The more common and more damaging kind is quieter and more internal, and most of the athletes who are affected by it don't think of it as selfishness at all.

It starts with the very natural, very human desire to be seen, valued, and recognized for what you contribute. That desire is not wrong. It becomes a problem when it starts directing your choices and reactions in ways that prioritize your individual visibility over the team's success.

It looks like the frustration that appears on your face — briefly, but visibly — when a teammate makes the play you could have made. Or the subtle withdrawal of energy that happens when the game plan doesn't feature you heavily and your attention starts to wander to your own role instead of staying locked on the collective mission. Or the effort fluctuation that correlates suspiciously with whether you're getting the recognition you feel you deserve. Or the halfhearted celebration when a teammate scores from a position you were competing for on the depth chart.

Nobody does these things intentionally. Nobody sits down and decides to be selfish in the name of selfishness. It happens because human beings are naturally ego-protective, especially in competitive environments where roles and recognition feel like limited resources. The selfish response is often the automatic response — the thing that happens when character and self-awareness aren't present to redirect it.

But here's what selfishness actually does to a team, beneath the surface: it erodes trust. Teammates can feel it — not always consciously, but viscerally. When someone is playing for himself even a percentage of the time, the cohesion changes. The willingness to go to battle for each other, to take the hard assignment, to sacrifice the individual moment for the team moment — it all gets slightly more transactional. Slightly more conditional. And transactional, conditional teams are fundamentally weaker than teams built on genuine mutual investment.

The Christian angle here is direct and worth being clear about: the entire logic of the gospel runs counter to self-promotion. The defining posture of Jesus was not greatness through accumulation but greatness through service. The one who wanted to be first had to become last. The leader took the lowest seat. Strength was expressed through giving, not grasping.

That is not a comfortable message for a competitive athlete. Competition involves wanting to win, wanting to be the best version of yourself, wanting to be in the game and making plays. That drive is not wrong. But the athlete who can hold that competitive drive and genuine team-first service simultaneously — who wants to be excellent and wants the team to win and understands that those two things are not in competition with each other — is the one who becomes genuinely great rather than just individually impressive.

## THE TEAMMATE YOU'RE RESENTING NEEDS YOU

Comparison in team sports has a particular flavor that is different from the individual comparison covered in Chapter 2. When you're comparing yourself to a teammate — someone you practice with daily, compete alongside, share a locker with — the comparison is more intimate and therefore more emotionally complicated.

You see his work ethic up close. You know exactly how hard he works and whether it's more or less than you. You know his weaknesses and his strengths because you've competed against him every day in practice. You have an extremely detailed, highly personalized comparison data set, and your brain processes it constantly, usually without you asking it to.

When the teammate you've been competing with for a starting spot gets the nod and you don't, the response is rarely simple. There's usually a mix: genuine support for him as a person, genuine disappointment about your own situation, and somewhere in there, depending on how honest you're being with yourself, something that feels uncomfortably close to resentment. Not at him, exactly. At the situation. At the outcome. At the fact that all the effort you put in didn't produce the result you were working for.

That resentment — even when it's mild, even when it's mostly suppressed — is spiritually and practically costly. Spiritually because it creates distance between you and a teammate who is actually your brother, who is doing the same things you're doing and wants the same things you want and deserves your genuine support. Practically because it is extremely difficult to compete at your full capability when part of your emotional energy is occupied by resentment. It divides your focus. It clouds your judgment about what the team needs. It makes you slightly less useful to everyone around you, including yourself.

The antidote to comparison and jealousy in a team context is one of the more demanding things this book will ask of you, and it is worth being honest about the difficulty: genuine celebration of others' success. Not performed happiness — real, honest-hearted happiness for a teammate who is doing well. Not in spite of the fact that his success makes your position more challenging, but including that fact. Choosing to genuinely root for him, compete hard for your own spot, and hold both of those things at once without letting either of them poison the other.

That is hard. It requires a security in your own identity and worth that doesn't need to be defended against a teammate's excellence. It requires the belief that his success doesn't diminish yours — which it doesn't, in any meaningful way, though it can feel like it does when performance-based identity is in play. It requires the kind of character that is bigger than the situation pressing on it.

That kind of character is built over time, through repeated choices. Every time you choose genuine support over hidden resentment, you're making a deposit into the kind of man you're becoming. It's not easy. It's worth it.

## WHY THE HUMBLE ATHLETE KEEPS GETTING BETTER

Humility gets a bad reputation in competitive sport because it gets confused with passivity. With not believing in yourself. With shrinking. With deferring when you should be asserting. With not having the fire to compete at the highest level.

That is a complete misunderstanding of what humility actually is, and it's worth correcting because the athletes who genuinely embody humility are often among the most competitive people in any room.

Humility is not the belief that you're not good. It's the accurate assessment of yourself — your strengths, your weaknesses, your current level, and the gap between where you are and where you want to be — without the distortion of ego either inflating or deflating the picture. Humble athletes know what they're good at, and they know what they need to work on. They're not pretending to be less capable than they are, and they're not pretending to be more.

What humility produces, practically, is coachability. The humble athlete hears correction as information rather than attack. When a coach says your footwork is off or you're not reading the defense correctly or your effort in practice this week has been below your standard — the humble athlete's response is: tell me more. What do I need to fix? That receptivity accelerates development at a rate that pride never matches, because pride's response to the same correction is: defend, justify, minimize, or deflect. Pride protects the ego at the cost of growth.

Humility also produces a kind of longevity. Athletes who are genuinely humble stay teachable across a career, continue to develop even after they've achieved significant success, and adapt when the game or their role changes. Athletes who are not humble hit a ceiling imposed by their own ego — they stop growing because they stop receiving the input that would take them further. The very success that should have given them the confidence to keep improving instead hardens into a fixed identity that resists further development.

In a team context, humility is the quality that makes you safe to be around. The humble teammate doesn't make his presence contingent on his role. He doesn't make the film session about whether his mistakes get mentioned or someone else's. He doesn't require special handling around his feelings. He can receive honest feedback, honest accountability, and honest assessment of the team's needs without making it about himself. That makes the people around him feel free — free to be honest, free to give correction, free to have the conversations that actually move the team forward.

*"Humble yourselves before the Lord, and he will lift you up." — **James 4:10***

The promise is significant. Not: humble yourself and suffer the consequences of being overlooked. But: humble yourself and be lifted. The path to genuine elevation runs through the willingness to not demand it. The athlete who needs to be the center of attention, who needs to be acknowledged for every contribution, who makes his cooperation conditional on recognition — that athlete's ceiling is lower than the one who serves freely and lets the results speak.

Genuine humility is not a weakness. It is a form of strength that is rare enough to be remarkable when you encounter it, and powerful enough to elevate everyone around it.

## HOW YOU RESPOND TO COACHING SAYS EVERYTHING

One of the most revealing tests of a young athlete's character is not how he responds to success. It's how he responds to coaching — specifically, to correction, criticism, tough love, and decisions that didn't go his way.

Coaches are human. They make mistakes, they have biases, they occasionally make lineup decisions that are wrong, and they sometimes communicate in ways that are less than ideal. It would be dishonest to pretend otherwise. Respecting a coach doesn't require believing he is perfect. It requires treating him with the dignity of his role even when you disagree with his decisions.

Here is what your response to coaching actually reveals. When a coach corrects you in front of your teammates and your instinctive response is to immediately explain yourself, to look away, to shut down, or to display visible irritation — that response tells everyone watching something about your maturity level. It says that your ego is more fragile than your game. It says that correction feels like an attack rather than an investment. And it says something to the coach about whether you are someone he can trust with honest feedback — which, over time, affects how much he gives you, and therefore how much you develop.

The response that builds trust is different. It's the direct eye contact that says I'm listening. The brief nod that says I got it. The effort on the very next rep that says I'm applying it. And if you genuinely disagree with something — a position, a decision, a piece of feedback that doesn't match your understanding of the situation — the appropriate response is a private conversation at an appropriate time, not a public display of disagreement in the middle of practice.

Receiving reduced playing time with maturity is one of the hardest things a competitive athlete can be asked to do. The instincts all run the other direction — argue, sulk, withdraw, transfer, question the coach's competence loudly to teammates. But here is the brutal truth about athletes who respond to reduced playing time with poor attitude: they almost always make it worse. Coaches do not respond to visible frustration by rewarding the frustrated athlete with more opportunity. They respond by losing trust in his emotional stability and keeping him on the bench until he demonstrates he can handle the situation like someone ready for more responsibility.

The athlete who handles reduced playing time with genuine composure — who keeps competing hard in practice, who keeps his attitude professional, who seeks feedback about what he can improve, and who does not make the locker room carry his disappointment — that athlete puts himself in the best possible position to earn his way back. And in the meantime, he is building the kind of emotional maturity that will serve him in every difficult situation the rest of his life.

Honoring coaches is not blind obedience. It's choosing to operate with respect within a structure, even when that structure is imperfect — which it always is, in sports and in every other area of organized human endeavor. That capacity is something you'll need constantly for the rest of your life. You'll work for imperfect bosses. You'll operate in imperfect systems. The young man who learns how to maintain respect and integrity within imperfect authority structures as a teen athlete is far better prepared for adult life than the one who has never learned to handle that tension.

# FOLLOWING CHRIST WHERE IT'S HARDEST TO FAKE IT

There is a version of Christian faith that is easy to maintain in low-stakes environments — at church, in comfortable conversations, in the presence of people who share your values and are not going to test them. That version of faith is real, but it's incomplete. Because faith that only holds up in comfortable conditions hasn't actually been tested.

The locker room is one of the most honest environments you will ever be in. Not because athletes are always brutally candid with each other — sometimes quite the opposite. But because the stakes are high, the pressure is real, the competition is personal, and the conditions are exactly the kind that bring out what people are actually made of. There is very little room for performance in a locker room. Your teammates see you every day, before the composure is fully assembled, in the moments when the frustration is raw and the exhaustion is real.

That means the locker room is one of the most important places your faith can show up. Not by being the guy who hands out Bible verses, not by making your Christianity a constant topic of conversation, but by living in a way that reflects the character of someone genuinely trying to follow Christ.

What does that look like in practice? It looks like the way you speak about teammates who aren't in the room — whether you protect their reputation or participate in the conversations that diminish them. It looks like the way you respond to the referee who made the call that cost you — whether you demonstrate self-control or join the environment of disrespect that sometimes spreads through benches and sidelines. It looks like the way you treat the least celebrated athlete on your team — the scout team player, the guy at the bottom of the depth chart, the freshman who is out of his depth and knows it. Does he feel like a valued member of the group when you're around?

It looks like honesty. Not brutal honesty weaponized as criticism, but the willingness to tell the truth — to a coach in a private conversation, to a teammate who is making poor decisions, to yourself about where your effort and attitude have been. Honesty, when it's delivered with care and appropriate timing, is a form of respect. It says: I think enough of you to tell you the truth instead of telling you what's convenient.

It looks like how you handle winning. Sportsmanship in victory is genuinely harder than sportsmanship in defeat for a lot of competitive athletes, because the instinct after winning is to celebrate — which is fine, natural, and appropriate — but the line between celebration and taunting, between joy and contempt for the opponent, is one that Christian character should guard carefully. Your opponents are also people. Their defeat is not an occasion for your contempt. Celebrate genuinely and respect them genuinely, and the athletes and coaches on the other side of the competition will notice.

*"Whatever you do, whether in word or deed, do it all in the name of the Lord Jesus, giving thanks to God the Father through him." — **Colossians 3:17***

In word or deed. The locker room is all word and deed. Every conversation, every choice, every reaction in competition — all of it falls under this instruction. That does not mean every action has to be a conscious theological statement. It means that the ongoing shaping of your character by your faith should produce behavior that, over time, reflects the Someone you're trying to follow. That's not a one-time achievement. It's a daily orientation.

# YOU'RE BUILDING THE CULTURE WHETHER YOU KNOW IT OR NOT

Team culture is one of those phrases that coaches use a lot and that sometimes feels abstract until you've experienced a team that has great culture and one that doesn't. Then the difference is completely concrete and impossible to miss.

A team with great culture feels different from the first day you walk into it. There is a standard of effort that nobody has to announce because everyone already knows it and holds each other to it. There is a way of treating mistakes — not with excessive harshness and not with dismissiveness, but with honest accountability and quick reset. There is a language of encouragement that flows without self-consciousness because it has become the normal currency of communication. There is a seriousness about the work that coexists with a genuine enjoyment of being around each other. Hard things get said honestly and received well because the trust level is high enough to sustain them.

A team with poor culture feels heavy in a different way. There is a fragility to the confidence — it swings dramatically with the last result. There are undercurrents of resentment and jealousy that never quite make it to the surface but that affect every interaction. Criticism, even well-intentioned, lands badly because the trust is not there to receive it cleanly. The effort is inconsistent because the standard is inconsistent. People are performing their commitment rather than actually living it.

Here is what most young athletes do not fully appreciate: they are contributing to one of those environments every single day, whether they intend to or not. Culture is not created only by coaches or captains. It is created by every person in the room, through every interaction, every day. The freshman who shows up with a great attitude and genuine effort immediately raises the standard. The senior who dogs it in practice and gets away with it immediately lowers it. The teammate who consistently encourages after mistakes makes the environment safer for everyone. The one who consistently says nothing, or worse, adds criticism at the wrong moment, makes it less safe.

You are building the culture. The question is what you're building.

That is not a burden — it's an opportunity. Because it means that a single athlete, committed to showing up with the right attitude and the right effort and the right treatment of others, has genuine influence over the environment around him. Not unlimited influence. Not magic influence. But real influence, the kind that compounds over time into something that becomes visible and eventually undeniable.

You do not have to wait for permission to start building. You do not have to be voted captain or officially designated as a leader. You just have to decide what you're going to contribute, and then contribute it, consistently, every day.

# YOU DON'T NEED A PATCH TO LEAD

Some of the most powerful leaders on teams have no formal title at all. They are not the captain. They are not the star. Sometimes they are not even starters. But when things get hard, when the game is going badly and the huddle needs something, people's eyes go to them instinctively. Because over time, through consistent behavior, they have built something that cannot be assigned or appointed: credibility.

Credibility is what you have when you have repeatedly done what you said you would do, when your behavior in hard moments has been consistent with your behavior in easy ones, when the people around you have enough evidence of your character to trust you when the pressure is highest. No coach can give you credibility. You build it yourself, slowly, through the accumulation of choices that nobody is formally scoring.

Leadership without a title looks like being the first person up after a team mistake — not to make a speech, but to reset your own body language and return to focus in a way that gives others permission to do the same. It looks like being the one who says the true thing in the film session that nobody wants to say but that everyone needs to hear, said with respect and without malice. It looks like checking on the teammate who is struggling, not because it's your job but because you noticed and you cared.

It looks like competing hard in the games that don't matter — the blowouts, the easy opponents, the practices when the coaches are distracted and it would be easy to coast. Not because anyone is evaluating you specifically in those moments, but because you have decided that the way you compete is not a function of the stakes. It is a function of who you are.

It looks like being consistently honest and consistently kind at the same time, which is harder than either alone. Kindness without honesty is flattery. Honesty without kindness is harshness. The athlete who can hold both — who tells the truth because he cares about the person he's telling it to, who delivers hard feedback in a way that lands as support rather than attack — is a genuinely rare and genuinely powerful presence in any team environment.

You do not have to wait for someone to give you this kind of leadership. You grow into it by choosing it, daily, whether or not anyone notices or responds. Some seasons the response will be visible — you'll see the team culture shift, see teammates follow your example, see coaches lean on you more. Some seasons it will feel like you're depositing into a bank account that never shows a balance. Either way, the deposit is real. It does not disappear. And eventually, in ways you may not be able to predict, it produces something.

# AN HONEST QUESTION

This section is going to ask you to do something that requires more honesty than most of the rest of this book: evaluate yourself in the context of your team, as accurately as you can manage.

Not harshly. Not as an exercise in self-criticism. But as an honest athlete's assessment of the kind of teammate and the kind of leader you are actually being — not the version you intend to be or the version you think of yourself as being, but the version your teammates and coaches actually experience day to day.

Think about the last week of practice. When things didn't go your way — a missed rep, a bad call, a stretch where someone else was getting the recognition — what did your attitude communicate? Did the people around you feel steadied by your presence or dragged down by it? Did your body language encourage or deflate?

Think about the last teammate who was struggling. Did you notice? Did you say anything? Not a speech — just something real. A word, a gesture, an acknowledgment that you saw them and you were still with them. Or did you stay focused on your own performance while they worked through it alone?

Think about the last time a coach corrected you in front of others. How did you receive it? Eye contact and acknowledgment? Or something that communicated, even subtly, that you were resistant?

Think about the teammate who is competing with you for playing time. When he has a good practice, when he makes the play that earns the coach's praise — what is your honest internal response? Genuine support? Managed resentment? Something in between?

These questions are not asked to produce guilt. They're asked to produce awareness. Because you cannot grow in the areas you haven't honestly assessed. And the young man who is willing to look at himself clearly — to see where his character is strong and where it still has gaps — is the one who actually closes those gaps over time.

# WOULD YOU WANT YOU ON YOUR TEAM? THAT'S THE QUESTION. BE HONEST ENOUGH TO ANSWER IT.

If the answer is mostly yes, with some areas to grow — that's honest. That's where most athletes are, and it's a good place to be if you're committed to the growth. If the answer has some uncomfortable patches in it — if there are specific ways your attitude, your selfishness, your comparison habits, or your response to authority have been costing your team something — that's important information. And it's information that you can do something with, starting today.

# THE LEGACY YOU'RE LEAVING IN THE LOCKER ROOM

Every team you are part of will eventually end. The season will close, the roster will change, people will move on. And what remains — what actually persists after the last game, after the last practice, after the final time the locker room empties out — is not the stats you accumulated. It's the impression you left on the people who were there.

Your teammates will remember how you made them feel. Whether you lifted them up or made them feel unseen. Whether you were someone they could trust in a hard moment or someone they had to manage around. Whether your presence made the team stronger or introduced friction that didn't need to be there. Whether you were the kind of teammate they wanted in the huddle when everything was on the line.

That legacy is being built right now. Not in the games, primarily — in the practices, the bus rides, the film sessions, the ordinary days when nothing important seems to be happening. It is built in the small decisions: the encouragement you choose to give, the selfishness you choose to set aside, the composure you choose to maintain when it costs something, the honesty you choose to offer when it would be easier to say nothing.

You have the capacity to be the kind of teammate that makes a team genuinely better. Not just because of your talent — though your talent matters. Because of your character. Because of the quality of your presence, the consistency of your attitude, the depth of your commitment to the people around you.

That kind of athlete is rare. Every team wants more of them. Every coach looks for them. Every team culture needs them. And that athlete is available to you — not because you were born with it, but because it is built, by choice, day after day, in the specific and ordinary moments of a season.

*"Each of you should use whatever gift you have received to serve others, as faithful stewards of God's grace in its various forms." — 1 Peter 4:10*

Faithful stewards of God's grace. That phrase, applied to your team context, means this: the ability you have been given — athletic, relational, emotional, the capacity for leadership and encouragement and composure — is not yours to hoard or to use primarily for your own benefit. It is a gift entrusted to you for the benefit of the people around you.

Using it that way is not a sacrifice of your individual development. It is the fullest expression of it. Because the athlete who gives his gifts in service of his team becomes more than an individual performer. He becomes a leader. And the leader who builds others up, who serves consistently, who holds the team together in hard moments — that young man is becoming something that outlasts any sport, any season, any scoreboard.

Build that. Starting in the next practice. The next huddle. The next moment you have a choice about what your presence is going to contribute.

Make it count.

# A PRAYER FOR THIS MOMENT

*God, I want to be honest: some of what I read in this chapter made me uncomfortable, because I recognized myself in it. The attitude on the bad days. The jealousy I didn't fully acknowledge. The encouragement I didn't give because I was too focused on my own performance. The correction I received but didn't really receive.*

*I want to be a better teammate than I have been. Not to get more recognition for it — but because I actually care about the people I compete with. Help me start to see them that way: as people worth serving, not just competitors to measure myself against.*

*Give me the humility to be coachable. The self-control to manage my attitude in the hard moments. The courage to encourage when it matters. The security to celebrate others without feeling diminished.*

*And help my faith show up where it's hardest to fake it — in the locker room, on the bus, in the film session, in the ordinary Tuesday practice when nothing feels important but everything actually is.*

*Make me a teammate others are grateful for. Amen.*

# THINK ON THIS

1. Think of the teammate on your team who most consistently makes the culture better. What specific things do they do? What can you learn from their example?

2. Where have your attitude and body language been costing your team something? Be specific. What would it look like to change that in the next practice?

3. Is there a teammate you have been quietly resenting or comparing yourself to? What would it look like to genuinely root for them this week while still competing hard for your own spot?

4. How do you typically respond when a coach corrects you? What does that response communicate to your coaches and teammates about your maturity?

# GAME-DAY CHALLENGE

This week, choose three specific leadership actions and execute them, regardless of whether anyone notices:

1. Encourage one teammate who is struggling — specifically, genuinely, and without expectation of anything in return. Not a generic "you've got this." Something specific and true.

2. The next time you receive correction from a coach, respond with direct eye contact, a nod, and immediate application on the next rep. No explanation, no defense, no visible frustration. Just: got it, and here's proof.

3. After the next practice, tell one teammate something specific you noticed them doing well. Not flattery — an honest observation. "I saw how you competed on that last drill. That was the standard."

These three actions cost nothing but attention and intention. Do them and notice how the people around you respond. Leadership is contagious when it's genuine.

# CHAPTER 6
# PLAYING FOR AN AUDIENCE OF ONE

PURPOSE, *Faith, and the Bigger Game*

*"Whatever you do, work at it with all your heart, as working for the Lord, not for human masters, since you know that you will receive an inheritance from the Lord as a reward. It is the Lord Christ you are serving." — **Colossians 3:23–24***

# THE THING YOU LOVE THAT CAN'T LOVE YOU BACK

Let's start with something honest.

You love your sport. Maybe that's an understatement. Maybe "love" barely covers what it is — the way it has shaped your schedule, your friendships, your sense of who you are, the way you think about the future. Some athletes describe their sport less like something they do and more like something they breathe. It is that central. That consuming. That close to the core of who they feel themselves to be.

That kind of love for a sport is not pathological. It's not something to be ashamed of or quickly corrected. It is, in many ways, one of the most powerful engines of athletic excellence — the depth of caring that keeps an athlete in the gym when everyone else has gone home, that makes one more repetition feel worth it, that sustains the discipline of the long and unglamorous middle of a season when the excitement of the opener has faded and the end is still a long way off.

Deep love for your sport is a feature, not a flaw.

But here is the tension worth naming honestly, because this whole book has been building toward it: sports, for all their power and importance and genuine goodness, cannot love you back. They cannot tell you that you matter when the scoreboard says you don't. They cannot hold you when the career is over and the uniform is retired and the world has moved on to the next athlete in line. They cannot answer the deepest questions about who you are and why you matter and what you are ultimately for.

Sports are an extraordinary gift. But they are not God. And the athlete who asks his sport to be both — to be a gift and a source of ultimate meaning simultaneously — will eventually discover that the sport is not equipped for the second job. It will fail at that assignment in the specific way that all created things fail when asked to carry the weight of something only the Creator was built to bear.

That failure usually hurts. It often comes at the worst possible time — after a career-defining loss, in the middle of a serious injury, in the slow realization that the dream is not going to unfold the way you mapped it. The athlete who has made his sport his god does not just lose a game in those moments. He loses the organizing center of his entire sense of self. And that is a specific kind of pain that no trophy, no scholarship, no comeback can fully address, because the problem was never the sport. The problem was asking the sport to be something it was never designed to be.

This chapter is about that. About holding the sport you love in the right hands — open hands, grateful hands, not clenched fists that grip it so tightly they can't feel anything else. About finding a purpose big enough to sustain you through all of it: the wins and losses, the seasons of recognition and seasons of obscurity, the years when the dream is unfolding and the years when it seems to be stalling out. About learning to play — really play, freely and fully — for an Audience of One.

# THE EXHAUSTING WORK OF MANAGING EVERYONE'S OPINION

There is a version of athletic life that an enormous number of teen athletes are living, and it is genuinely exhausting — though most of them are too deep inside it to see it clearly from the outside.

It goes something like this. Before the game, the primary emotional driver is not excitement about competing. It is anxiety about how you will be perceived. By the coach who evaluates your future on this team. By the parent in the stands who has invested significantly in your development. By the teammates who are watching to see if you deliver. By the social media audience who will see the highlights. By the recruiter who may or may not be watching. By the opposing players who will know whether you were as good as advertised.

During the game, the internal monologue is not primarily about execution. It is about perception management. How did that play look? What is the coach thinking? Did my teammates see that mistake? Is the crowd reacting in a way that tells me how I'm doing? Am I living up to the expectations of the people watching?

After the game, the primary emotional process is not reflection on what you learned and what you want to build on. It is the anxious monitoring of feedback. What did the coach say? How did people react? What are people posting? What did my parents say on the way home? Was the consensus positive enough to feel like I did okay?

That is not competing. That is performing for a jury whose verdict is never final and whose standards keep shifting. It is one of the most anxiety-producing ways a human being can move through the world, and it is remarkably common among athletes who have never been given a different framework.

The fundamental problem with approval-seeking is that approval is an inherently unstable currency. The same crowd that cheers wildly for you one game will go quiet if you struggle the next. The same coach who praised you this week will be harder on you when the stakes rise. The same social media following that responds enthusiastically to your highlight will scroll past your ordinary Tuesday without noticing. Human approval is real, it's pleasant when it's present, and it tells you something genuine about your performance. But it is not a foundation. It fluctuates too much, depends on too many variables you can't control, and provides too little of what you're actually looking for when you go looking for it.

What you're actually looking for when you seek approval is not really other people's opinions. It's the answer to a deeper question: am I okay? Am I enough? Do I matter? And those questions cannot be answered by the crowd, no matter how loud the cheer.

*You will never perform your way into the approval that actually satisfies, because the approval that satisfies doesn't come from a crowd.*

The athlete who understands this — really understands it, in the place where it changes behavior rather than just sounds good — is the one who starts to compete differently. Not less intensely. Not with less care about performance. But from a different source of motivation, aimed at a different destination.

# WHAT IT MEANS TO PLAY FOR AN AUDIENCE OF ONE

Playing for an Audience of One is a phrase that gets used in Christian sports culture often enough that it can start to feel like a slogan — familiar, pleasant, and somewhat easy to nod at without letting it actually change anything. So let's slow down and get specific about what it actually means in the real context of your real athletic life.

It does not mean that the opinions of coaches, teammates, and fans stop mattering. They do matter, in appropriate ways. Coaching feedback is valuable. Teammates' trust is something worth earning. Doing well in front of people you respect is a genuine joy. None of that is wrong.

Playing for an Audience of One means that God's perspective on your effort, your attitude, your character, and your purpose is the primary reference point — the evaluation that matters most deeply, the one that your peace is ultimately anchored to, the one that holds when every other audience has left the building.

It means that when you play well and nobody notices, you are not empty-handed. The One who matters most noticed. It means that when you play with integrity and honesty in a moment where cutting a corner would have been invisible to everyone else, there is an audience for that too. It means that when the hardest moment of your athletic life arrives — the injury, the end of the dream, the season that didn't go the way you worked for — your foundation is not your performance reputation, which is fragile. It is your relationship with God, which is not.

What does playing for an Audience of One look like in practice, in the specific moments of a competing athlete's life?

It looks like giving your full effort in the practice where no scouts are watching, no parents are in the stands, and it would be completely invisible if you coasted — because you have decided that your effort is an offering, and the offering doesn't require an audience to be real.

It looks like maintaining your character in the postgame conversation with an opponent who is being disrespectful — because you are not playing to the crowd's response to that conversation. You are playing to a standard that has nothing to do with how cool it makes you look to respond in kind.

It looks like the way you treat the least visible person on your team — the scout team player, the manager, the freshman who barely makes practice because of other obligations — because your treatment of people who can do nothing for your reputation is one of the truest measures of your character, and the Audience of One sees it even when no one else does.

It looks like the peace you feel after a hard loss when you honestly know you gave everything you had and competed with integrity — not because the loss doesn't hurt, but because the evaluation that most matters has already come back favorable. You played for the right reason, in the right way, with the right heart. That is enough. Not in a passive, indifferent way — in the deeply satisfying way that comes from knowing you were genuinely faithful to the calling of this moment.

*"Am I now trying to win the approval of human beings, or of God? Or am I trying to please people? If I were still trying to please people, I would not be a servant of Christ."*
**— Galatians 1:10**

Paul's framing is sharp and worth sitting with. The question is not whether human approval matters at all — Paul clearly cared about the people he served and worked hard to communicate effectively with them. The question is what sits at the center. What is the primary aim? If pleasing people is the primary aim, the result is a life that shifts with every wind of opinion, that has no stable reference point, that is perpetually anxious about the latest verdict from the latest audience.

But if serving Christ — living and competing in a way that honors the One for whom you're ultimately doing this — is the primary aim, then human approval becomes something pleasant when it comes and non-catastrophic when it doesn't. It loses its power to be the thing your peace depends on. And in that loss, something more stable and more satisfying takes its place.

# WHY WINNING IS NOT A BIG ENOUGH GOD

This might be the most counterintuitive idea in this entire book for a competitive athlete: winning, by itself, is not enough. And the further along you go in competition, the more clearly you can see this truth — because at higher levels, the athletes who have already won a great deal are among the people who most clearly demonstrate what happens when winning becomes the organizing center of a person's life.

Here is the pattern. An athlete works incredibly hard toward a specific goal. Wins the championship, gets the scholarship, makes the team, earns the starting spot, achieves the thing they have been building toward. The moment of achievement is genuinely wonderful. The feeling is real and worth celebrating. And then, with remarkable speed, something shifts.

The new standard arrives. Now that you have done this, the next thing needs to happen. The championship needs to be defended. The scholarship needs to be justified. The starting spot needs to be maintained. The achievement that was the destination becomes the new starting line, and the satisfaction that was supposed to arrive with it turns out to have been briefer and less stable than you expected.

This is not a character flaw. It is a feature of human psychology called the hedonic treadmill — the tendency for the emotional impact of positive events to fade quickly, returning us to roughly the same baseline we had before the event. The win that you have been working toward for two years will produce approximately six hours to six days of genuine happiness. Then the baseline reasserts itself, the new pressure arrives, and the old anxiety begins to rebuild.

That cycle is not the enemy of ambition. Ambition is good. The pursuit of excellence is worth sustaining. The problem is when winning is not just a goal but an identity — when you are trying to win not just the game but the existential question of whether you matter, whether you're enough, whether your life has value. Because that question cannot be answered by a scoreboard. And the athlete who keeps trying to answer it that way will spend an entire career being briefly satisfied and perpetually restless.

There is a reason that some of the most famous athletes in history — people who achieved everything their sport had to offer — have spoken openly about the emptiness that arrived when the achievement was complete. Not because winning is meaningless, but because winning is not the thing they were actually looking for. The achievement answered the athletic question. It couldn't answer the deeper one.

The deeper question has a deeper answer. And no trophy is the right shape for it.

*"What good is it for someone to gain the whole world, yet forfeit their soul?"* — **Mark 8:36**

Jesus asked that question two thousand years before anyone invented sports performance analytics, and it has lost none of its precision. What good is it? Not: winning is bad. Not: excellence is wrong. But: what does it profit you to accumulate everything the world offers as a measure of success, if the thing at the center — the soul, the self, the identity that has to live with what you've become — is lost in the process?

The athlete who keeps winning is not automatically the one who is most okay. The athlete who builds something real and lasting — in his character, his faith, his relationships, his sense of purpose — while he competes is the one who will have something to stand on when the competition is over and the crowd has gone home.

# SPORTS AS A GIFT YOU RECEIVE, NOT A GOD YOU SERVE

Here's a way of thinking about sports that might reframe things significantly: a gift and a god require fundamentally different postures from the person who holds them.

A gift is received with open hands and gratitude. It is appreciated, used well, enjoyed deeply, and held loosely — because gifts can be given and taken away, and the giving and the taking away are both in the hands of the giver, not the receiver. A gift enriches your life. It does not define your worth. And when the gift is eventually returned or changed or removed, the person who received it as a gift grieves the loss genuinely but remains fundamentally intact — because their identity was never dependent on the gift.

A god is something entirely different. A god is something you organize your life around, something you make sacrifices for, something you look to for ultimate meaning and worth. A god demands from you rather than giving to you. A god's approval is never permanently secured — there is always another sacrifice required, always another standard to meet, always another risk of falling out of favor. And when a god fails you — when the thing you organized your life around doesn't deliver what you needed it to — the damage is not just disappointment. It is a collapse of the organizing structure of your entire existence.

Sports, held as a gift, are extraordinary. The physicality, the competition, the teamwork, the discipline, the pressure, the joy of excellence, the deep satisfaction of hard work that pays off — these are genuinely wonderful things. They shape character, build resilience, create community, and provide a context for some of the most meaningful experiences of a young person's life. Sports as a gift are worth loving deeply and working for fiercely.

Sports, held as a god, are a setup for a specific kind of pain. Because gods that are made out of created things — out of performance and recognition and success — are inherently fragile. They can be taken away by injury, by age, by a coach's decision, by a single bad game at the wrong time. And when they are taken away, the person who organized his entire identity around them is left with nothing to stand on.

The posture this book has been building toward — through every chapter — is the open-hands posture. Competing with everything you have, caring deeply, working with all your discipline and focus and heart — and holding the whole thing as something that was given to you, not something you earned the right to possess permanently. Grateful for the opportunity to play, honest about the limitations of what playing can provide, and rooted in something strong enough to hold even if the gift is eventually taken back.

*Hold your sport with open hands. Give it everything you have. Just don't let it own what it was never meant to own.*

That is not a passive posture. It is one of the most demanding things this book will ask of you, because it runs directly against the natural human tendency to grip the things you love most tightly — especially when they feel like they might be slipping away. Open hands are more vulnerable than clenched fists. But they're also more free. And an athlete with open hands can receive more, give more, and ultimately experience more than one who is spending his energy gripping.

## THE LONGER ARC: WHAT YOU'RE ACTUALLY BUILDING

One of the gifts of youth sports — one that is easy to miss when you are inside it — is that they are not primarily about the results. They are about formation. About what is being built in you through the experience of competing, preparing, struggling, winning, losing, recovering, leading, following, pressing on.

The trophies, if they come, are real. The stats are real. The scholarship is a genuinely significant opportunity and a legitimate goal to work toward. None of that is being dismissed here. But the trophies will sit on a shelf and eventually be packed in a box. The stats will be forgotten by most people within five years of the final game. Even the scholarship, significant as it is, is a door to what comes next rather than the destination itself.

What does not go on a shelf or get forgotten is the character that was built through the athletic experience. The discipline you developed because you showed up when you didn't feel like it, for years. The resilience you built because you faced real pressure and real failure and came back from both. The humility you grew through being corrected and receiving coaching over a long period. The leadership you learned through the experience of being trusted with the welfare of a team. The faith you developed because you were in enough pressure situations to discover, firsthand, that you are not the source of your own strength.

That formation is not incidental to your athletic career. It is the most valuable product of it. The athlete who finishes his competitive years not just with performance memories but with a deeply formed character — one that has been tested, refined, and proven through the experience of real competition — has received something that will compound in value for the rest of his life.

Purpose, viewed through that lens, is not about where you finish in the standings. It is about who you are becoming through the process of competing. And that process is available to every athlete, regardless of level, regardless of outcome. The third-string player who competes with full integrity, who builds genuine discipline, who serves his team faithfully through a season where his name never appeared in the box score — that athlete is building something real. Something that will show up later, in contexts that have nothing to do with sports, in ways that will matter far more than any statistic.

*"And we know that in all things God works for the good of those who love him, who have been called according to his purpose." — **Romans 8:28***

All things. Not just the winning things. Not just the seasons when the dream is unfolding on schedule and everything is going right. All things — including the hard seasons, the obscure seasons, the seasons of injury and disappointment and waiting. God is working in those. Not despite the difficulty, but through it. Building something in you that the easy seasons could never build alone.

Your purpose in sports is not to win everything. It is to become someone through the experience of competing. And that purpose is available in every season — the great ones and the devastating ones — because the formation is not conditional on the outcome.

# WHAT FAITH DOES WHEN NOBODY IS WATCHING YOUR HIGHLIGHTS

Every athlete will have hidden seasons. Seasons that don't feel like they count — the injury year, the redshirt season, the stretch where you're doing everything right and the results are not reflecting it, the time between a chapter that has ended and a new one that hasn't quite started yet. Hidden seasons are not exciting. They are not the material of highlight reels or inspirational posters. They are often genuinely painful in their ordinariness, in the specific disappointment of working hard in circumstances that feel invisible.

And they are among the most important seasons of an athlete's formation.

Because hidden seasons are where faith is tested at its most basic level. When the outcome is visible and positive, faith is easy to maintain — gratitude flows naturally, the sense that God is good and present is reinforced by the surrounding evidence. When the outcome is invisible or negative, faith has to survive on something other than evidence. It has to survive on conviction — the settled belief that God is working even when nothing visible confirms it, that purpose is present even when it can't be seen, that the formation is happening even when it feels like stagnation.

The athlete who has built genuine faith before the hidden season arrives will experience that season very differently from the one who has treated faith as a pleasant addition to athletic success. The first athlete enters the difficult stretch with a foundation that holds because it was built before it was needed. The second discovers in the difficulty that the foundation was shallower than it appeared.

This is one of the practical arguments for the daily spiritual habits discussed in Chapter 4 — the consistent, unglamorous, low-stakes practice of prayer, Scripture, and honest conversation with God that happens regardless of how the season is going. Those habits build the kind of faith that holds in the hidden seasons. Not because they are magic, but because the relationship they maintain with God is deep enough to sustain the strain of circumstances that would otherwise sever it.

The injured athlete who cannot play, who sits on the sideline watching his team and wondering what his future looks like, who faces the specific uncertainty of a body that is not doing what it was built to do — that athlete can still have purpose. Not despite the injury, but within it. The purpose of learning patience. Of discovering the depth of his love for the game in the painful absence of it. Of being present to teammates in a way his playing schedule never allowed. Of building the kind of faith that can survive the worst athletic experiences and come out the other side intact.

None of that makes the injury pleasant. None of it means the hidden season is secretly great. It means that purpose does not take a season off. It shows up wherever the athlete is willing to look for it.

*"Consider it pure joy, my brothers and sisters, whenever you face trials of many kinds, because you know that the testing of your faith produces perseverance. Let perseverance finish its work so that you may be mature and complete, not lacking anything." —* **James 1:2–4**

Mature and complete, not lacking anything. That is the destination that the hidden seasons are contributing to. Not the trophy case, not the stat line — the complete person, the one whose faith and character have been tested enough times that they are genuinely solid. That person is not built only in the glory seasons. He is built especially in the hidden ones.

## THE QUESTION EVERY ATHLETE EVENTUALLY HAS TO ANSWER

There will come a day — specific, real, not as far away as it feels right now — when you play your last game. For some athletes it comes at eighteen, when high school ends and the path to college competition doesn't materialize the way they hoped. For some it comes at twenty-two, at the end of a college career. For a very small number it extends into professional sport. But for everyone, it comes.

And on the day after that last game — the day when the jersey is retired, the routine is gone, and the structure that organized your entire week for the last decade or more suddenly isn't there anymore — a question surfaces that is either answered or devastating, depending on what you built during the playing years.

The question is simply: who am I now?

For the athlete who built his entire identity on the sport, this question has no good answer available. The sport was the identity. Without it, there's a gap — sometimes a yawning, disorienting, genuinely distressing gap that nobody warned him about and that nothing in his athletic preparation helped him anticipate. Athletes who retire from sport, especially athletes who were deeply invested in their identity as athletes, experience rates of depression, anxiety, and purposelessness that are significantly higher than the general population.

Not because they are weak. Because they are untethered. Because the thing that answered the identity question for their entire adolescence and young adulthood is no longer available, and they don't have a deeper answer ready.

This is not meant to be frightening. It is meant to be a reason — a very practical, very concrete reason — to build identity on something that doesn't end with the final whistle. Not at the expense of your athletic ambition. Not as a reason to care less about your sport. But as a reason to invest, right now, in the parts of yourself that will still be present and growing and meaningful when the sport is a memory.

Your faith. Your character. Your relationships. Your capacity to lead, to serve, to give to others, to be honest, to work hard at things that matter. The habits of mind and heart and spirit that you are building right now, in the middle of your athletic career — those do not retire. They compound. They transfer into everything that comes after sport and make that everything richer, more stable, and more meaningful.

The athlete who finishes his playing years and can say: I am someone who knows how to work hard, how to bounce back, how to lead, how to serve, how to hold things loosely, how to trust God in difficulty, how to be genuinely present for the people in my life — that athlete has won something that goes on a shelf that never fills up and never gets dusty. He has won the formation of a person who is ready for whatever comes next.

That is the thing worth building. And you are in the middle of building it right now, whether you know it or not. The question is whether you are building it intentionally.

# THERE IS A BIGGER GAME BEING PLAYED

Your sport takes place inside a boundary. Lines on a field, walls around a court, lanes in a pool. The competition is real, the effort is real, the outcomes matter genuinely. But your life is not bounded by those lines. The bigger game of your life is playing out simultaneously, in every direction — in who you are becoming, in how you treat people, in what you build in the decades ahead.

The bigger game includes your faith — the ongoing, growing, tested relationship with God that is being formed right now through every experience, athletic and otherwise, that this season is delivering.

It includes your character — the person who is being built in the hidden moments, the private habits, the quality of your effort when nobody is evaluating it, the way you respond to difficulty and success and everything in between.

It includes your relationships — the teammates you are choosing to genuinely invest in, the coaches you are honoring with your respect even when they make decisions you don't agree with, the family members who are showing up for you in ways that deserve more acknowledgment than they usually get.

It includes your influence — the younger athletes who are already watching how you carry yourself, the peers who are forming their own understanding of what competitive masculinity looks like based in part on what they observe in you, the people in your community who are seeing what a young man of faith looks like in action.

It includes your future — the adult you are becoming, the husband and father and professional and neighbor and citizen who is being built right now from the raw material of how you are choosing to live. That person is not a future project. He is being assembled today.

The bigger game is already in progress. And the formation that is happening in it — through all of it, including the sport you love so much — is the truest measure of the season you are having.

*The scoreboard measures one game. Character measures a life. Only one of those keeps mattering after the final whistle.*

God is not primarily interested in your stats. He is profoundly interested in your soul — in the specific, irreplaceable, eternally significant person you are and are becoming. The sport you play is one context in which that person is being formed. It is a significant context, a rich one, one that God can and does use in remarkable ways. But it is a context, not the content. The content is you — your faith, your character, your love, your purpose, your life.

Play the sport with everything you have. And keep your eyes open to the bigger game that it is contained within.

## PLAY HARD. PLAY FREE. PLAY FOR SOMETHING THAT LASTS.

Here is the vision this book has been building toward, and it is worth saying it clearly now that all the pieces are on the table:

You can care deeply about your sport without being owned by it. You can compete with ferocious intensity without needing the outcome to tell you who you are. You can want to win with everything in you while playing from a foundation that holds even if you don't. You can give full effort, full discipline, full heart — and still hold the whole thing with open, grateful hands.

That is not a contradiction. That is, in fact, the only athletic posture that produces both genuine excellence and genuine peace. Because the athlete who is playing from a settled identity, with a clear purpose, for an Audience whose approval is already secured — that athlete plays free. He plays brave. He plays with the specific kind of joy that belongs to someone who is doing exactly what he was made to do, with nothing to prove and everything to give.

That is a different experience of competition than the one driven by anxiety and approval-seeking. It doesn't mean the pressure disappears — pressure is part of competition, and a settled identity doesn't eliminate adrenaline. It means the pressure no longer carries existential weight. It is the productive pressure of a challenging situation that you are genuinely prepared for and genuinely present to — not the crushing pressure of someone whose worth is riding on the result.

Play hard. Compete with discipline and excellence and genuine intensity. Want to win and work for it and grieve genuinely when it doesn't come. Those things are good and right and worth keeping.

But play free. Free from the need to perform for any audience other than the One who already knows your name, already values you completely, and will still be your foundation on the day after the last game of your career. Free from the identity fragility that makes every bad play feel like a personal verdict. Free from the approval addiction that makes the crowd's response the measure of your worth. Free to give everything you have to the people around you, to the team you're part of, to the competition you're engaged in — because you're not holding any of it back in reserve to protect yourself.

And play with purpose. Not the shallow purpose of accumulating recognition, but the deep purpose of becoming someone. Of honoring the gift you've been given with the full use of it. Of competing in a way that reflects the character of someone who is genuinely trying to follow Christ — in the locker room, on the field, in the film session, in the hard moments and the ordinary ones. Of understanding that the bigger game is always in progress, and that every choice you make inside the lines is a choice you're making inside the bigger game too.

That is the athlete this book has been trying to help you become. Not the most impressive stats or the most decorated career — though excellence is worth pursuing with everything you have. But the most fully alive, most fully grounded, most fully purposeful version of you that this sport and this faith and this season can produce.

# THE LAST THING THIS BOOK WANTS YOU TO CARRY

You picked up this book — or someone who loves you picked it up for you — because something about your athletic life needed something that sports alone couldn't give. Maybe it was the pressure. Maybe it was the identity struggle. Maybe it was the habit of bouncing too hard off mistakes. Maybe it was the comparison, the slump, the confidence that felt too fragile for the moments that demanded it. Maybe it was the quiet sense that something important was missing from the way you were competing and the way you were living.

Every chapter of this book has been trying to address some version of that missing piece. The pressure that can be held without being crushed by it, because the foundation beneath you is more stable than the scoreboard. The identity that doesn't rise and fall with the last result, because it was established before the first game was ever played. The resilience that bounces back from mistakes without being broken by them, because grace is bigger than failure. The discipline that builds something real in the hidden moments. The character that makes a team better and leaves a legacy in the locker room. And now this — the purpose that makes all of it mean something beyond the trophies and stats and recognition.

None of it is complicated. It is simple — though simple is not the same as easy, and every piece of it requires ongoing commitment to practice and apply. But the core of it can be said plainly:

You are made by God. You are known by name. Your worth is settled and secure and was established before you ever competed for anything. The sport you love is a gift — a genuinely wonderful gift worth giving your full effort to — but it is not your god and it is not your identity. You play free because there is nothing the scoreboard can take from you that actually belongs to it. You compete hard because excellence honors the One who gave you the ability to compete at all. You bounce back from failure because grace is real and it covers your worst moments. You build habits because character matters and small things compound into large ones. You invest in your teammates because they are people, not just competitors in a system. And you hold it all — the sport, the dreams, the effort, the outcomes — with open hands, in the presence of a God who is with you in all of it.

That is the bigger game. It started before your first season and it will continue after your last one. And how you play it — not just in your sport, but in your life — is the thing that matters most and lasts longest.

Go play your sport with everything you have.

Go play your life with everything you have.

And do both of them for an Audience of One — the One who was watching before anyone else arrived, and who will still be there when everyone else has gone home.

# A PRAYER FOR THIS MOMENT

*God, I want to lay something down right now — the weight of trying to earn my worth through performance, of living for everyone else's approval, of asking my sport to answer questions it was never built to answer.*

*I love this game. You know that. But I don't want it to be my god. I don't want my peace to be this fragile, this dependent on how the last game went or what the coach said or how the crowd responded. I want something more stable than that.*

*Help me play for You. Not perfectly — I know I'll drift back toward approval-seeking, and I'll need to be redirected. But help me make You the primary Audience. Help me compete with the freedom of someone whose identity is already settled.*

*Give me a bigger vision for what this sport is actually building in me. Help me see the hidden seasons as formation, not waste. Help me care about who I'm becoming as much as I care about what I'm achieving.*

*And when the day comes that the sport is over — however that day arrives — let me be the person who walks off the field with something real. Something that doesn't fit on a trophy but that lasts forever.*

*I'm Yours. Before the game starts and after it ends. That's enough. Amen.*

## THINK ON THIS

1. Be honest: whose approval are you most anxious about when you compete? What does that tell you about where you're looking for worth?

2. If you removed all external recognition from your sport — no stats, no coaches' praise, no social media, no crowd — would you still play with the same effort and joy? What does your answer reveal?

3. What is your sport actually building in you, beyond athletic performance? What character qualities are being formed through the experience of competing?

4. Who will you be when the jersey comes off? What are you building right now — in your faith, character, and relationships — that will still be there when the sport is a memory?

## GAME-DAY CHALLENGE

This week, try the Audience of One experiment for one full practice or game:

Before you compete, set a single intention that has nothing to do with outcome or impression: "I'm going to play this one for God — full effort, full integrity, full gratitude for the ability to be here."

During the session, every time you notice yourself playing for the crowd, the coach, or your own approval-anxiety, gently redirect: back to effort, back to purpose, back to the Audience of One.

After the session, evaluate on a different scale than usual. Not: how did I perform? But: did I compete with integrity? Did I give everything I had? Did I honor the gift? Was my character consistent with who I want to be?

That evaluation, done honestly, will tell you something about how you actually feel when the purpose of your effort is in the right place.

You might be surprised how free it feels.

# YOU'RE JUST GETTING STARTED

*Conclusion*

*"Being confident of this, that he who began a good work in you will carry it on to completion until the day of Christ Jesus." — **Philippians 1:6***

## LOOK AT WHERE YOU STARTED

Think back to where you were when you picked up this book.

Maybe you were dealing with the specific, familiar weight of performance anxiety — that tight chest before the big game, the sleepless night of worst-case scenarios, the sense that your worth was somehow on the line every time you competed. Maybe you were fresh off a bad game, carrying the emotional aftermath through a week of practice and school and family dinners, wondering why you couldn't just shake it off the way everyone kept telling you to. Maybe the slump was happening, or the bench, or the quiet but corrosive comparison to a teammate who seemed to be getting everything you felt you were working just as hard for.

Maybe you didn't have a specific crisis. Maybe you just had a vague sense that the way you were competing wasn't as free as it should be. That something was heavier than it needed to be. That there had to be a better way to hold all of this — the sport you love, the pressure it carries, the questions it raises about who you are and what you're worth — without being exhausted by it all the time.

Whatever brought you here, you came. And that matters.

Reading a book about your mental and spiritual life as an athlete is not the automatic move for most teen athletes. It requires a kind of honesty — a willingness to acknowledge that the way things have been going is not quite the way you want them to go, and that something needs to be added or changed or built. That honesty is itself a form of strength. And you showed it just by being here.

Now look at what you've been given through these chapters.

You've been given a different way of understanding pressure — not as a signal that something is wrong with you, but as a signal that something matters to you, and as a place where courage, not fear, gets to make the decision about how you respond. You've been given a different foundation for your identity — not the scoreboard, not the stat line, not the coach's current opinion of you, but the unchanging declaration of a God who knew you before you ever competed for anything. You've been given a framework for bouncing back — the acknowledge, release, redirect, and return-to-truth sequence that can interrupt a spiral before it becomes a bad half, a bad game, a bad week.

You've been given the truth about discipline — that confidence is not manufactured from thin air, but built from the honest accumulation of preparation and effort in the hidden moments. You've been given a vision for what your influence on a team can look like when character leads the way. And you've been given the deepest truth of all: that there is a bigger game being played, one that outlasts any sport, any season, any career — and that you are in the middle of playing it right now, in every choice, every habit, every relationship, and every moment of integrity when nobody is watching.

None of that is small. All of it is real. And all of it is available to you now in a way it wasn't before.

## THE ATHLETE, AND THE MAN, YOU ARE BECOMING

Let me describe someone for you.

He walks into a big game with nerves — because he cares, and caring produces nerves, and that's okay — but underneath the nerves there's something steady. A foundation that the outcome can't move. He knows who he is before the whistle blows, and the whistle doesn't get to change that. So he plays free. Not fearless — free. There's a difference, and he lives inside it.

When he makes a mistake — and he does, because all athletes do, because perfection was never the standard — he acknowledges it briefly, releases it cleanly, and redirects his attention to the next play. Not because the mistake didn't matter. Because he has learned that dragging the last play into the next one is a choice, and he has chosen differently. The spiral is shorter now. The recovery is faster. The next play stays clean.

He competes hard. Full effort, full discipline, full intensity. He wants to win with everything he has. But his worth is not riding on the result. So when a hard loss comes — and hard losses come for everyone — he feels it genuinely and processes it honestly and comes back to work with his identity intact. He grieves the loss without being defined by it. He learns from it without being destroyed by it. And he comes back.

In the locker room, his presence makes the environment better. Not because he delivers speeches, but because the consistency of his attitude, the quality of his effort, and the way he treats people — the starting quarterback and the last man on the roster equally — creates a culture of trust. His body language communicates even when he says nothing. He encourages specifically and genuinely. He receives coaching without defensiveness. He is the kind of teammate others want in the huddle when everything is on the line.

He builds his habits in private. He shows up when it's not exciting. He prepares because he has learned that honest preparation is one of the greatest gifts he can give himself on game day. And he carries his spiritual habits alongside his athletic ones — the morning check-in, the brief honest prayer, the Scripture that speaks to what he is actually carrying that week — not because it makes him feel super spiritual, but because those habits keep him connected to the foundation that everything else is built on.

He plays for an Audience of One. He competes with gratitude for the gift of being able to compete at all. He holds his sport with open hands — giving it everything, releasing the grip that turns a gift into a god. And he carries a vision of purpose that goes beyond any single season, any single scoreboard, any single moment of recognition or disappointment.

That is the athlete and the young man this book has been trying to help you become.

You are not fully there yet. Neither is anyone else. But you are on the way. And the way you are on — the one that runs through honest faith, genuine discipline, resilient character, and the deep security of knowing who you are before any game has been played — is the right one.

# THE WORK ISN'T DONE. THAT'S THE POINT.

This book is not a certificate of completion. You don't finish the last page and graduate into an athlete who never struggles with pressure again, who is permanently free from comparison, who bounces back from every mistake with effortless composure, who never has a bad day or a hard season.

That is not the outcome of any book. That is not the outcome of any amount of growth. The pressure will come back. The spiral will try again. There will be games where your identity feels more fragile than you want it to, where the comparison bites harder than you remembered, where the discipline slips and the bad habits reassert themselves. There will be seasons that are genuinely difficult in ways that no amount of mental preparation can make comfortable.

What is different now is not the absence of those things. It is what you bring to them when they arrive.

You bring a framework for understanding pressure that stops it from being proof that something is wrong with you. You bring a foundation for identity that the scoreboard cannot reach. You bring a reset process for mistakes that shortens the spiral and returns you to the present. You bring an understanding of discipline that connects daily effort to long-term confidence. You bring a vision of leadership that sees your influence on others as something worth taking seriously. And you bring a purpose that is bigger than any single season — one that is not diminished by a bad game or a lost role or a hard year.

That is more than you had before. And it compounds. Every time you use these tools in a real situation — every time you choose the next play over the spiral, choose discipline over the shortcut, choose genuine encouragement over hidden resentment, choose to play for the Audience of One when the crowd is pulling you somewhere else — you are reinforcing the neural pathways and the character patterns that make the next difficult situation easier to navigate.

Growth is not a destination. It is a direction. And you are pointed in the right one.

## THIS IS BIGGER THAN SPORTS. YOU ALREADY KNEW THAT.

Everything you have learned in this book translates. Directly, specifically, powerfully — into every other area of your life that involves effort, pressure, failure, comparison, and the question of where your worth comes from.

The mental toughness you build under athletic pressure will be the same mental toughness you draw on when the job interview is hard, when the relationship hits a difficult stretch, when the adult responsibility lands on your shoulders and the stakes feel impossibly high. The discipline of showing up consistently when you don't feel like it — the habit that makes you a better athlete — will make you a better student, a better employee, a better husband, a better father. The character you are building in the hidden moments of athletic life is the character that will define everything that comes after it.

The identity you are establishing — the one that doesn't depend on performance for its security — will protect you in every environment that evaluates and compares and ranks. The workplace does that. Relationships do that. Social media is basically nothing but that. The young man who enters those environments with a settled sense of who he is and where his worth comes from is not immune to the pressure. But he is not at its mercy either. He has a foundation that those environments cannot shake, because it was built before they had the chance to define him.

The resilience you develop by bouncing back from athletic failure will be the same resilience that carries you through the adult failures that are coming — because adult life delivers genuine, significant failures, and the only question is whether you will be someone who can absorb them and come back, or someone who has never learned to do that.

The humility and coachability you practice with coaches and teammates will be the humility that makes you developable in every future context — the employee who keeps growing because he stays teachable, the leader who builds great teams because he is not too proud to receive input, the man whose relationships deepen over time because he can actually hear the people who love him.

And the faith — the daily, consistent, sometimes-gritty practice of staying connected to God through the ordinary and the extraordinary — will be the anchor that holds through everything. Not a faith that is only present on game day or in crisis. A faith that is woven into the fabric of daily life, practiced in the unglamorous moments, deepened by the hard seasons, and ultimately more real and more solid than anything the world can offer as a substitute.

*The athlete you are becoming is preparation for the man you are becoming. And both of them matter — forever.*

## STAY WITH IT WHEN THE SEASON CHANGES

One of the patterns that is easy to fall into as an athlete is treating faith as a resource you pull on when things are hard. The injury happens, and you pray. The pressure peaks, and you read Scripture. The slump arrives, and you reach for God. And all of that is completely right — those are exactly the moments when faith needs to show up, and you should absolutely bring them to God.

But faith that only shows up in emergencies is like a muscle that only gets worked under maximum load. It's not ready. It doesn't have the depth or the flexibility or the reserves that consistent daily practice builds. And when the emergency passes and the pressure eases and the season gets good again, the tendency is to ease off the spiritual habits too — to treat them as situational tools rather than foundational practices.

The young men who build genuinely deep faith — the kind that holds through the hardest things life delivers, the kind that produces the peace and courage and identity security this book has been describing — are the ones who practice consistently. Not perfectly. Not dramatically. Consistently. The brief morning check-in. The honest conversation with God at the end of a hard day. The willingness to bring the real stuff — the frustration, the fear, the uncertainty, the gratitude — rather than performing a cleaned-up version of yourself in prayer.

God is not surprised by your hard days, your bad games, your doubts, or your inconsistency. He is not impressed by polished performances of faith and unimpressed by the raw version. He wants the honest version. The regular, messy, genuine presence of a person who keeps showing up — not because they have it all together, but because they have decided that the relationship matters more than the image.

Stay with it through the winning seasons and the losing ones. Through the seasons when faith feels electric and the seasons when it feels like discipline with no immediate emotional payoff. Through the big game weeks and the ordinary Tuesdays when nothing important seems to be at stake. The consistency of your faith practices across all of those conditions is what builds the depth that holds when you need it most.

God is faithful even when you are not. But the young man who chooses faithfulness consistently — in the small daily practices, in the honest ongoing conversation, in the regular return to Scripture and prayer and gratitude — becomes someone who experiences that faithfulness at a depth that seasons of inconsistency never quite reach.

## HERE IS THE CHALLENGE

This is the part where I ask something of you.

Not because you owe it to this book, and not because the request comes with any guarantee of a particular outcome. But because everything you've read means very little if it stays only in your head — if it remains a set of ideas that you thought were interesting and then went on with the old patterns.

The challenge is to carry this into the next practice. The next game. The next hard moment. To actually use the tools when the situation calls for them — not perfectly, not without struggle, but with genuine intention.

When the pressure hits before the big game, take the breath, say the brief honest prayer, and choose to stand on the foundation instead of the anxiety. When the mistake happens and the spiral starts, run the reset. Acknowledge, release, redirect, truth. Let the next play be clean.

When the comparison bites and a teammate's success feels threatening, catch the resentment before it roots. Remember that his win doesn't take anything from yours. Choose to root for him genuinely, compete hard for your own spot, and hold both of those things without letting either poison the other.

When the discipline is hard and the motivation is absent and the easy path is right there — choose the harder thing. Not because it always feels good. Because you have decided what you are building, and you have decided that the building matters more than the comfort of not building today.

When a coach corrects you, make eye contact. Nod. Apply it. When a teammate is struggling, say the specific true thing. When someone easier to overlook needs to feel seen — see them.

And when the season ends — however it ends, whether it goes the way you dreamed or not — walk off the field knowing that you competed for something bigger than the result. That the Audience who matters most was watching. That you gave what you had, with integrity, with courage, with gratitude, for the right reasons.

That is the challenge. Not a perfect season. A purposeful one.

## YOU WERE MADE FOR THIS

You were not made to be crushed by pressure. You were made to be shaped by it. To develop courage through it. To discover, in the middle of the heat, that the foundation beneath you is exactly as solid as you needed it to be.

You were not made to measure your worth by a scoreboard. You were made — known by name, before the first game was ever played — with a worth that no result can confirm or deny. That worth is not on the table every time you compete. It was settled long before the competition started.

You were not made to play it safe with the gift you've been given. You were made to compete with everything you have, freely and bravely and fully, from the security of knowing that the outcome belongs to God and the effort belongs to you — and that giving your genuine best is an act of honoring the One who gave you the ability to compete at all.

You were not made to navigate this alone. The God who made you is the same God who is with you in the locker room, in the pressure moments, in the hard seasons, in the quiet Tuesday practices when nothing seems to matter and everything actually does. He is not watching from a distance, evaluating your performance with a clipboard. He is present — in the specific, personal, unmistakable way of a God who knows your name — and He is for you.

The pages of this book are behind you. The work is ahead. And the work is good.

Go compete. Go build. Go lead. Go grow.

Go be the athlete and the young man that everything you've read here was written to help you become.

The bigger game is in progress. You are in it. God is with you in it.

Play free.

## GO. YOU'VE GOT THIS.

When pressure comes — choose courage.
  When you fail — choose the next play.
  When comparison bites — choose security.
  When discipline is hard — choose to build.
  When your team needs someone — choose to lead.
  When the crowd is loud — remember the Audience of One.
  And in all of it — remember who you are.

## A FINAL PRAYER OVER YOU

*God, thank You for this athlete. For the specific, irreplaceable, already-complete way You made him. For the gift of his ability, his competitiveness, his drive, his capacity to care so deeply about something.*

*As he closes this book and goes back to the field, the court, the track, the weight room — go with him. Be present in the pressure. Be his foundation in the moments when the scoreboard tries to tell him who he is. Be his reset when the spiral starts. Be his peace when the nerves are loudest.*

*Build in him the kind of faith that holds not just in the big moments, but in the ordinary ones — the Tuesday practices, the quiet preparation, the daily habits that nobody else sees but You do.*

*Give him the courage to compete freely. The discipline to prepare honestly. The humility to stay teachable. The resilience to come back from hard moments. The character to make every team he is part of better.*

*Help him hold his sport with open hands — giving it everything, gripping it as a gift rather than a god. Help him compete for the right audience. Help him remember, even when everything is loud and fast and pressurized, that his worth was settled before the game started.*

*And when this season ends and the next one begins — in sports, in school, in work, in life — let the formation that happened here keep going. Let the character keep compounding. Let the faith keep deepening. Let the man keep becoming.*

*He is Yours. Before the first game and after the last one. That is more than enough.*

*Amen.*